THE SEARCH FOR THE GOOSE'S PALM

Simon Greene

ISBN: 978-1-326-50985-9

PublishNation
www.publishnation.co.uk

"The world is your lobster."

Arthur Edward Daley *(R.I.P.)*

PROLOGUE

I Have a Dream

So there I was, sprawled across an ageing Chesterfield in a sparsely filled darkened Luton boozer with a few of my motley crew, when the conversation turned to me. For mid-week, It had been a historic night of hardened drinking with heated discussions on Bupa v the NHS, science v religion and FIFA 15 v Subbuteo. I had filled in the pauses in the debate, between the drinking and arguing, looking for sympathy with lightened tales of my adventures, including hard luck stories of my current financial predicament.

"Good sir, if I might be as bold to make a suggestion, the answer to your woes lies in a book." Said a double for Phineas Fogg, stepping from the shadows of the fireplace. "Uh," he continued. "Yes, a publication of one's travel journals."

"Not now mate, maybe in eighty days!" I joked.

His face returned to the flames. I moved away to order one for the road. Strange, I thought, it's not April the first is it?

Standing directly in front of me at the bar stood a veteran female dressed for Wimbledon; she was ordering a mixed double. So I moved my forehand between her waist and the next bloke to create a space at the counter. 'The next bloke,' some idiot sitting on a stool sporting a Kangol hat, was chatting with some artist looking geezer who I noticed only had one ear. I asked him to move his easel, but he ignored me. Ignorant fucker I thought, and as they were blocking my path, I asserted myself by barging into them.

"Oh, excuse me lads." I said acrimoniously.

The post-impressionist soon pissed off, but the hat on the bar stool loudly reversed, and screeched to a halt right on my toe. It stood up and turned. Oh shit! It was only the menacing Samuel L. Jackson, and he looked in the most of reverent of moods.

"WTF is he doing in our pub?" Crossed my mind while hopping on the spot.

He pursed his lips, and then with ominously pointing finger; he thundered "I've been listening to your bullshit for two hours now dog, so here's some friendly advice. What's yo name boy?"

"Simon Greene." I replied in a voice smaller than usual.

"Well Greene, now I'm not saying that your book is gonna

be the next Lonely Planet, or even popular like you's the son of that Wicker man."

"He didn't have one; that's why they burned him," interrupted the tennis player.

"Say what bitch?" Said Jackson, somewhat thunderstruck that someone had dared interrupt.

"The Wicker man; he was a virgin. That's why they burnt him." She continued.

"No, not that motherfucker," said Jackson. "I'm talking 'bout the limey TV presenter, Alan Wicker, same as the other travelling Brit, Monty. No. What's his fucking name? Er Palin."

"It's Michael . . . Jackson," said the veteran tennis player, firstly selecting her glasses then a track from the walled mini Juke box.

"Incorrect, lady."

"No, I mean it's Michael as in the first name of Jackson, but not you, Jackson," she said.

Confusion turned to realisation as Jackson said with a vexed smile, "Well thank you, Billy fucking Jean!"

He then shook his head and sat down sucking on clenched teeth, and turning to the no-nonsense landlady behind the bar said, "Yo lady, guess it's too late to go get me a Royale with cheese and a regular coke?"

"Come again, love?" She replied. "Where do ya think this is Honey Bun, bloody Jack Rabbit Slims? Look, pal, this is Wednesday, not West Side."

The landlady tutted and flicked her peroxided bob, then reading from the small menu began.

"Right, love, we got chips in gravy; that's fries to you Yanks or cheese 'n onion crisps. Which apparently are chips, all very confusing. Oh, and there's some faggots, that's. . ."

"Hey, bitch don't even go there." Interrupted Jackson.

"Oi, anymore of your American profanities Mr Jackson and I will be saying goodnight, and we spell that N-I-G-H-T, understand pal?"

I hadn't eaten all day except for the dentist's favourite, a pork scratching, so I sneaked a few fries from Jackson's plate. Luckily he was busy discussing Amsterdam coffee shops with Van Gogh while I waited for my Amstel. He suddenly turned, and caught me, oh shit. Time for another sermon.

"Yo Greene, thieving is not the way brother, behold the Gospel of St John (the last supper).

"Go write your book dog, aim to be da buffalo soldier. . . Not da Judas Charmers!"

"Boom boom." Interrupted the landlady.

"Hey, you all wrong bitch," said Jackson grinding his teeth again and this time looking extremely pissed. He stood up again and looked me in the eye. Then poked my chest.

"Let me tell you, Greene . . . always seize the moment, fortune favours the brave. Remember dog, the pen is damn mightier than the sword, you dig?"

"Not according to the lady in the lake," said Gandalf the

Grey, appearing in a flash. Jackson became enraged at all the constant interruptions. I twisted my nose off to check this was all real, yep, that's definitely my snot. The bar had become totally surreal; it was like being backstage at a pantomime. As Hobbits and half-lings sang songs about The Bedfordshire.

Jackson suddenly snapped and leapt up, grabbing Gandalf by the beard, and with belligerent tongue, said, "That was Merlin, motherfucker; you's in the wrong Wizard movie!"

He then pulled a Saturday night special from inside his jacket, puffed out his chest and stood up on his stool to address his by now silent and attentive audience.

"Now, listen me good, this goes out to all you apostate two-bit heathen honky fuckers, and as I said in Jackie Brown, my arse may be dumb, but I ain't no dumbass motherfucker. You see; the path of the righteous man is beset on all sides by the iniquities of the selfish and the tyranny of evil men. Blessed is he who, in the name of charity and good will, shepherds the weak through the valley of darkness, for he is truly his brother's keeper and the finder of lost children. And I will strike down upon thee with great vengeance and furious anger those who would attempt to poison and destroy my brothers. And you will know my name is the Lord when I lay my vengeance upon thee."

Bewildered by this evening's recreation, and not wanting the proverbial cap in the arse, I downed my pint and stumbled out into the starry night with his mate, Van Gogh.

"Fancy sharing a kebab Vincent?" "Na, I'll walk thanks."

"Uh?"

Once upon a time

I opened my eyes and sat up, Jesus, what a dream and so vivid, this was biblical, was it a message, a calling? As a dream, it was up there with Martin Luther's or at least Bobby from Dallas. Plus with an endorsement, from the coolest actor on the planet. Twenty minutes later I was staring at my PC monitor with bacon sandwich in gob. I immediately typed. Once upon a time. . .

The cursor repeatedly flashed, then the screen wrote, "Well come on then!" Shit, I thought, this thing is far easier said than done!

So what is a good book? Well I suppose it must contain a collage of tragedy, history, comedy and drama. Maybe I could rip of Shakespeare? After all, this book is a comedy of errors. The bottom line is that friends have advised me on many occasions to transfer my storytelling and narratives onto a page in return for some wedge. Although they find some of my tales, as indeed you probably will, quite remarkable, they had enjoyed feasting on my humorous fables and assure me financial rewards were waiting from a Mr WH Smith or in the Amazon (junction 13, not the jungle).

Look, I don't dispute I have some amusing stories to tell and yes, maybe over the years I've sprinkled them with a bit of pixie dust. Some might say (especially Liam) that I flowered them up a bit. Well, that's because when one narrates one's own experiences, it's inevitable that one will add a layer of self-raising on occasions. Look, pal, basically they are all true. Definitely. Maybe.

The Seed

I always dreamed of travel and when my brother joined P&O Cruises and sent home huge postcards from giant countries, I knew Magaluf would never be good enough. I think even as a kid I was subconsciously attracted to travelling. As I remember, I loved to watch geography programs or films shot on location in far away places. Most of my childhood was spent over the backfield or in the park kicking footballs, so consequently school work suffered.

I replaced my academic shortcomings at school with being the class clown. Now we all know there are hundreds if not thousands of kids just like me, who fuck up their exams for the expense of getting a laugh, trying to be popular. Unfortunately, most people are laughing at you, and not with you, as I find even in later life. You may think you're funny, but it's not true that we will all become stand-ups or say a young Stephen Fry and live a hedonistic life and still get a triple blue with honours. For that, you need a clever pair of your father's genes. My Dad wore overalls!

Now, I'm not saying I was thick, far from it. I had the usual comprehensive education but foolishly chose not to take part.

I could tie my shoelaces at three, read a clock at four, sing football chants at five. What else do you need? Oh yeah, a few GCSE's wouldn't have gone amiss.

"Don't waste your school days boy, they will come back to haunt you." Cried England's finest headmasters. Yeah, but I didn't have Dumbledore, more like a dumb arse bore.

"I'm 18 with a bullet, got my finger on the trigger, gonna pull it." Sings some bloke from my Phillips transistor. Not quite, I thought, but it's getting close. I was sitting in the local park swigging 5% apple juice with my girlfriend, and trying to persuade her to give me a tug; an apter version of the song would have been. "I'm 15 with a Bulmers; she's got her finger on my Woodpecker gonna pull it." I wonder if Peter Wingfield played doctors and nurses?

I reloaded my potato canon as I was holding Barbie hostage, but Ken is a no show. Fuck it! So I'm thinking, this ain't fun anymore, it ain't even Cider with Rosie! I'm just another bored teenager, and my piggy bank's starving, time for an escape plan son. So join the Navy, she says! Fuck off.

Fast forward eighteen months. It's 1977 and anarchy is in the UK. So with hair spiked and looking pretty vacant, methinks it's time to see the world. Right now. Ha ha ha ha ha.

"I am an Antichrist; I am an anarchist. Don't know what I want, but I know how to get it, I wanna destroy passerby. . ."

Although I loved the music and the image, I didn't necessarily agree with the sentiment. Nevertheless those were exciting days filled with sex and drugs, not forgetting the buzz of boozy football days. So what else could there be?

THE SEARCH FOR THE GOOSE'S PALM

CHAPTER 1

Travel

I think that enjoyment of travel comes from some deep urge to explore. As a famous saint once said, "The world is a book, and those who do not travel read only page one." Not sure if it was Augustine or Sir Roger Moore.

I soon found out that to become an intrepid explorer required money, so at seventeen I took a labouring job, but saving was impossible as I had just discovered pubs and older girls. All this meant that life's pleasures became a financial struggle and would require the digging of extra holes (OT) to avoid the disappointment of missing out on teenage kicks. Being skint when young is probably compulsory in life, but in my Adrian Mole days, I had become an entrepreneur with school days often quite profitable.

Myself and Dave, who was and still is, my best mate, had set up various money making schemes at Stopsley High School in Luton to enhance our pocket, paper round and dinner money. The first was a lunchtime card school with a snide pack. The coppers soon mounted up to silver then notes, and we put them to good work purchasing and then flogging cigarettes behind the bike sheds. We sold singles or 3's tied up in a rubber band to the fifth-years. However, even with our casino winnings we couldn't meet the demand because our senior buyer, Baki Morris (17), wasn't always available. Luckily one night someone left the doors to the local working mans' club open, and the keys to the vending machines.

The word was out; pupils were even turning up at my house desperate for fags. I agreed to swap one dippy kid 40 Embassy Sovereign for his Dad's Yamaha. Later I thought "What the fuck am I gonna do with an organ?" Having presumed it was a motorbike!

Our next business enterprise was to entice a fourth-year girl to offer her services to the first year oinks, i.e., for a snog or a tit up. Patricia Boole was unloved except by her wicked step brother; she was half St Trinians, half Anne of Green Gables, and half flea bag, ("injection for life") and as an exhibitionist. . . . Hang on a minute that's one and a half! Listen, before you start to boo. She was more than happy to do her strip routine for a 20% cut, ten number 6 and extra Wagon Wheels. But then suddenly she was expelled, for head-butting Mr Ballcock, the swimming teacher, who's breaststroke had reached too far.

Sticky Mayfair and Titbits took her place, but they never

quite had the appeal of Ms Boole. Our crowning glory was when we made a tenner by charging kids ten pence to see Malcolm Hills' enormous shit.

He was a 'grebo' styled fifth year with W. G. Grace beard and dirty leathers, and the only kid at school who totally understood both meanings of AC/DC, even the teachers were scared of him. One day, he donated a historic dump to the science block toilets. It was gigantic. A man-made monument and a must see attraction, worthy of a pilgrimage and nearer than the Post Office Tower.

The queue to see "Tarka the Otter" almost reached Dunstable, and it even attracted CND but unfortunately also Mr Gilmere, who promptly roped it off and called the UXB squad.

Dave then found a major money supply with another one of our mates, working in the fruit & veg market. Somehow lots of pictures of Florence Nightingale found their way into his socks, but after six months his salad days ended when the other coppers mounted up. One fateful Saturday the high life became the high jump after the CID hid behind the plums.

Pernicious Advice

In my post-school infancy, my travels were normally funded by a black horse, but I soon realised overdraughts don't work, just ask the third world and Greece! So I dumped Lloyds and decided that I needed to acquire other skills of living beyond my means. This involves getting some beans from somewhere, but don't sell your cow, for, unlike Jack, there is no golden egg. (Except in Arndale Centres) and gambling is a sure way of getting nothing for something.

So what then? Well, saving for a rainy day takes forever in Britain's climate. So I would advocate plastic.

Get yourself an 18th birthday card from Barclay's or one of the million lenders out there. Look, back in the day I could have slowly joined the rat-race instead of the rat-pack by boarding the bus to boredom, but I decided to sell my spunk to the devil after meeting a man in a pub one rainy afternoon. He explained the world of finance to me. "There's plenty of time for cardiac infarction and a life in grey-scale," he said. "Why spend every day worrying about tomorrow when you can borrow?"

At only nineteen, I thought he seemed to have a point. Especially the two sticking out the top of his head! I mean nowadays there are all sorts of options, and if it all goes wrong you can always buy a puppy and move into a shop doorway, "Ai bani de rezerva?" That means, "Got any got any spare change, mate?" In Romanian.

But be sure not to fall for the "knock, knock" trick. "Knock, knock." "Who's there?" Thought you said you were homeless?"

Meanwhile back to Lucifer and me in the pub. "Listen, Simon," he continued, "90% of you would like a castle in Windsor with red prancing ponies on the drive and various designer clobber. Some of your mates may even wish for a free sherbert, but you should stick with a suitcase and plastic because unless your were born with a silver spoon mate or turn to crime, dream on pal, you ain't gonna win the football pools. And if you must tie yourself down, try S&M. I have various chambers at reasonable rates.

So. Burn the candle my lad, at both ends, and I'll see you downstairs in thirty years when the wick runs out."

The Unscrupulous Plan

Taking the advice of Nick, I applied for a Visa, no, not that one, well not yet, this one's got a hologram. Look a credit card is the gateway to Atlantis, so go fill it up and don't pay it back, who cares, it's not your money right? Anyone who lives within their means suffers from lack of imagination.

Wrong. I got my first card at 18 and rewrote a few Who lyrics, I was born with a plastic card in my mouth, but I didn't die before I got old.

I progressed into a real-life game of Monopoly. Take the ship, not the iron; that's for your wife, and in hindsight use loaded dice, as I landed on chance a few too many times. In fact, ignore the last paragraph, like I should have fucking done. OK, I wasn't perfect, but better the Devil you know. My reckless behaviour has lately resulted in mugging Peter to pay Paul all too often, and he's getting rather pissed off.

It all sounds great when you play Monopoly with someone else's money. But subsequently if you're playing on a Monday morning, you will see that eventually you will land on a hotel in Mayfair like I did. Now in my fifties with two young children trying to find the sofa to hide behind every time the bell rings is no way to live, especially after the bailiffs already took it. Next week I'm going down to Georgia to have a word with the Devil.

So Forget travel. As if. Look, the only real piece of advice I would ever give anyone is just try to see a bit before you go west. Oh, and take a clean pair of underpants.

But if I still can't tempt you, then fair enough, save your stash and re-creosote your fence.

Last and least, if you do find yourself in a similar predicament to me nowadays, one piece of financial advice I would advocate is taking a tip from the Greek Parliament. If a debt collector does turn up, just tell them your name's Spiros Papadopoulos and give him Chancellor Merkel's email! B.T.W. I wonder if I qualify for PPI?

CHAPTER 2

Anchors Aweigh

When Oscar Wilde said, "Youth is wasted on the young," he wasn't talking about me, I already had an old head on rounded shoulders. On the whole, our trips were more than the usual lad invasions, childish and high-spirited granted, but we were just young men looking for excitement, and although we never courted trouble, it normally found us. You could say we were the original Inbetweeners and yes, you could say we were also idiots abroad and yes, we were indeed often wasted. But so was Wilde.

By the time I became 30 something, and sheriff fat man,

I had already lived Annie Lennox's sweet dreams, and I had travelled the world and the seven seas. But not backpacker style, living off noodles and saving Nemo. You see I had already served my time in the Blackpools of the Med with the Frankie says brigade. I knew now it was time to trade my Umbro shirt, white socks and Simple Mind for World Party and a Gordon Gecko suit.

I went to proper places and met regular people, staying at the finest hotels, sipping Moet in business, or on one occasion Cristal in first. In other words, my numerous trips became a mongering rock 'n roll life of luxury for at least eight weeks a year.

I became anyone I liked, living a bit like Frank Abagnale (in Catch Me If You Can) but without breaking the law. People at work would slag my money wasting and lavish lifestyle through jealousy and not having the bottle or good sense to trade their four-berth shitbox in for two weeks in Barbados.

In my mid-life years, I solved 'the crisis' by clocking up more flying hours than Captain Kirk. Then I decided to open up warp drive and leave our shores and boldly went to S.E. Asia, where I lived and worked for ten years (that's another book!)

Dear reader, this book is by no means a literary masterpiece that's gonna be reviewed by Melvin Bragg, and Don Quixote it ain't. It's just a light-hearted look at some of my adventures along the yellow brick road. I have tried to write the chapters as if I were telling you the stories down the pub. Any advice I offer should be taken with a large pinch of Saxo.

I freely admit some of the humour is irreverent, infantile, even implausible and, like an overcooked fondue, it sometimes whiffs of cheese. I guarantee it occurred. Many references and characterisations derive from film, TV and music; I'll leave the poetic descriptions to Shakespeare again, or Pam Ayres, and thank fuck for spell chick. Over the pages are highlights of just a few lengthy narratives that you will not find on Trip Advisor.

Some people say you make your own luck in life, but I knew I was going to be unlucky when at the age of five I found a penny and lost my pocket money. My life of being behind the eight ball steadily progressed, culminating with a visit to a temple in Macau in 1997 where a Kau Cim, aka the local sooth-sayer, threw my chosen holy sticks onto their edge. Which is apparently unheard of.

"This is worse than bad luck, or a curse Pigsy." Said Tripitaka, my boyish priest translator, in a scene from eighties TV series, *Monkey*. The Kau Cim then danced around me as if I was the Hungry Ghost, chanting her prognostication of "Listen Pal, you can't have your fortune cookie or eat it." Then, throwing fire crackers at me, she finished with "You're going down with the Villa!"

"Dragon's shit." Was my reply, only to be called almost instantly by my house-sitter in the UK informing me that I'd been burgled.

Life has generally continued in the same vein since, for me and the Villa. Regrettably I have now resettled into UK life, rejoining the repetitious indifference of existence.

More importantly today, I realise reciting my stories and great voyages to my mates; Wilson, the listening rabbit, and the Polish at the sausage counter; doesn't actually help feed my family, so thank you for purchasing my book.

At least it can't get any worse!

Knock, knock. Bang, bang, bang . . ." WTF?

"Shit dad, hide, it's Tom Hanks!"

CHAPTER 3

The Wonder Years

A collection of sophomoric stories from my youth

Sometimes I still feel like an immature idiot inside, but nowadays I look in the mirror and see this old guy who keeps getting in the way.

Summer Loving

Ring, ring. "Hello, Luton 21039," said mum in her posh telephone voice, in fact, her everyday voice. . .

"May I ask who's calling? Could you hold on, please. Simon, here a minute," said mum in a slightly louder voice, from the bottom of the stairs. "It's Keith on the telephone."

I kicked a football at Rex, our German goalkeeping shepherd, who failed to save it yet again, and subsequently was red carded by dad for breaking his tenth ornament that month. Rex was a great dog and the younger brother I never had, and very useful for ravaging my foes or blaming for all my house trashing. I sometimes reflect if a bite he inflicted on me in his later years was equitable vengeance.

"Coming." I replied.

"Hello?"

"Si, I've found us a caravan to rent in the Vauxhall Mirror, it's only £7.50 for the week," said Keith in an enthusiastic manner.

"Wow, errrrrrr where?"

"Nacton."

"Where? Clacton?"

"No, Nacton. . . 6 miles South of Lowestoft."

Hardly tropical, I thought and, despite scouring the Thompsons and Cosmos summer brochures, In my heart I knew they wouldn't have any Spanish deals left at costa tenner. Anyway, at 16 anywhere would do really for our first parentless holiday. Luckily as a kid in the seventies I'd been overseas several times, and although mum and dad couldn't really afford it, they left saucy postcard guest houses to Mrs Mycroft at number four. This all meant I wasn't that knowledgeable on knobbly knee resorts but come on Keith. . . Lowestoft: Yarmouth on a Tuesday in February.

Having said all that, I do remember we did do Butlins when I was about seven. I particularly remember seeing a large red and white sign in a field from our car window it had some funny foreign language next to "Welcome to Wales." Wow I'm in a different country, I thought, as a cow stood next to it with tail in air unloading a steaming volley of Desperate Dan's lunch. It's funny, I still get faint flashbacks of concentration camp potato salad and skinheads at Pwllheli when I hear *Groovin with Mr Bloe*. Hi di hi.

Keith, I, and the rest of class 5JP were all in the process of leaving Stopsley Senior School in Luton; all the other kids were still being reluctantly dragged off by their parents wearing kiss me quick hats but not us. As I said, we were about to embark on our first parentless lads' holiday, we managed to hatch an extremely cunning pre-Baldrick plan. Which was that I would be holidaying in Norfolk with Keith's parents and vice-versa. We paid a local girl called Olive Saunders, who was nearly eighteen, fourteen pence in coppers including expenses, to call them from a phone box. We chose her because she was battle axe hardened, wore bottle rimmed specs and doubled for her namesake from TV's *On the Buses* and, more importantly, she sounded like Sue from the Sooty show. Amazingly they fell for it, even if she did call them Mr Corbett. Although it was more likely, they wanted a week to rest from anal teenagers.

I only ever saw Olive once more some years later in motorcycle and sidecar.

Putting this story on pause for just a moment it wasn't strictly true that it was my first holiday alone. Also, I'd taken school trips out of the equation; like Stow on the Wold where I got sent home for pushing Harold Ivy accidentally on purpose off a bridge. Base jumping in its infancy. I did take part in two forced expeditions without mummy and daddy, but as they were heavily chaperoned, I'm not counting them. The first occurred at 14 when I was abducted by the Christian Youth Army and taken to the Isle Of Wight. Unfortunately, they failed to save me, and I have hated the fucking tambourine ever since.

The second was a two-week action-man government inflicted scheme, aka the Duke of Edinburgh's outward bound course at Ullswater, where I was subjected to an assault course of rock climbing, canoeing, raft building, pot holing and army hikes. . . Instead of going to borstal. I roomed with a collection of Britain's elite from Milford School including the sons of the ruling classes and celebrities. One comic book lad named Baby face Tarquin, who's bollocks were yet to drop, was also blessed with a speech impediment . . . "Shank you shyman for sharing your shpangels widtch me." Ironically he was the offspring of a chat show host.

Surprisingly most of them failed miserably at the outdoor life and spent most of their time pleading on the telephone to be allowed to come home. I thought they were supposed to be Tom Brown, toughened up from playing rugger, being thrashed by Flashman and piercing boils with Matron. However, their red cross parent parcels from home contained boxes of Aeros and Toffee Crisps and were a very welcome addition to midnight feasts in hut Seven and helped keep our strength up for the customary tunnel digging under the wood stove. I decided to team up with Tarquin because he had the largest tuck box. He was 13 years old and from Leeds. Apparently his grandfather was a self-made shithouse millionaire 'thy knows there's brass in muck' kinda fellow, his older brother Sebastian, also on the course was heavily into Buddhism and tried to convert our hut with promising of Curly Wurlies if we reached enlightenment.

Most of our gang were in awe of Seb because he was tall, confident, with chiselled breeding and around 16 and twenty-three days, but I had him well sussed, fucking Grasshopper . . . he kept boasting about he was at one with nature and the mountains then on Tuesday slipped off Hellvellin peak and broke his leg.

I was also befriended by a copper running the course, who seemed a decent bloke and tried to teach me the error of my delinquent ways which had sent me there. I realised later that to shower twice a day with our hut was not in the brochure, in fact, I included it in my end of course essay entitled The Secret Adventures of Hut Seven by P. C. Blyton. . . But nothing came of it.

The school was set up by Norgay "Sherpa" Tenzing and Sir Edmond Hillary, a couple of chaps who went up a big hill once. One morning I thought I heard Tarquin say that Tenzing had arrived. I ran excitedly to inform the lads, but it turned out my deciphering of lisp-language was incorrect and instead of meeting a fifties icon arriving we collectively witnessed the arrival of a Sherpa van full of tents.

For my gallant efforts, I received an award of a gold medal

and a letter from Phil the Greek and yeah, it did toughen me up a bit. It takes bottle to crawl 100 meters through a two-foot cave tunnel half full of freezing water in the pitch black roped to Lord Snooty. "Rock on Tarquin." I shouted.

Meanwhile back to the story. . . A week prior to the Nacton knees up, Keith and I travelled by bus to Leighton Buzzard and met up with the caravan owner, a Mrs Granny Gralton. We assured her everything would be OK and after showing her a typed letter of reference from a fictitious scout master, she handed over the keys. I threw her a salute and a few dib dib dobs, hoovered her cat then told her blind husband had won the sun bingo. We then proceeded to the nearest pub where then I experienced my first serious session.

I remember drinking port and black and sliding down the bar and then somehow later reversing the charges to my dad 15 miles away to come and rescue me. Of course, I repaid him for the favour by throwing up in his new Vauxhall Viva all the way home. I thought I was dying. You know when you get that really awful feeling like you've being lost in Star Trek's transporter room? For fuck's sake Scotty. I woke up several times in an alcohol induced delirium during the night, reliving Dumbo's Fantasia experience when he fell in the wine vat. At midday, I surfaced with him still sitting on my head and Jimminy Cricket flying round my Mateus Rose lamp.

We left on the bus with four older girls, i.e., cans of Tennants and allegedly about a fiver each. Turned out Keith only had one pound, 70p and ponced off me for Shippams potted paste sandwiches, No. 6 and Ice breakers that I supplied. Although he did manage to nick some butter beans from the camp shop, but we didn't have a tin opener, and as there were only about 12 people in the park, we couldn't be arsed to knock around for implements to open a can of bland vegetables.

The site was an aluminium graveyard with scary weather to match. Our caravan resembled school rice pudding; white, cold and lumpy. The East coast wind ripped right through you, despite being sheltered by an inlet. There was a swimming pool especially for shopping trolleys and a so-called beach which resembled a sand-pit, but the location made reaching it the equivalent of a D-Day landing. The clubhouse was pretty empty most nights, but we managed to pinch cafe creme and bottles of Cherry B around the back. The music acts were so awful that in later years while watching Phoenix Nights, I swear I'd seen most of them before. One night they had a Roger Whittaker tribute band. Well one bloke on guitar and his bird on basket weaving. On Saturday night was the disco that we decided was to be our holiday's saving grace.

We were told that the local banjo playing youth came down from the surrounding hills by the VG stores manager, Burt Reynolds, who also stood on Keith's foot and told him not to squeal like pig. Oh, what to wear? Did they have fashion in deepest Norfolk? Probably, but turned out we were in Suffolk. My mate Keith was still in flares and winkle-pickers, and had a bit of a fifties rock n' roll affiliation, so he was social club PC. But I grew up listening to my brother's record collection, The Who, Stones, Zeppelin, Faces and now punk and looked for bands to go to see in the New Musical Express. Keith was Showaddywaddy, Mud, Racey and other shite and looked for wanking material in the People's Friend.

Keith was tall and skinny with a neck twitch that resembled a pigeon dancing to ska. So off we set. Keith, stop starting, the big bopper with Vaselined Dove's arse. Me in my new Kings Road(ish) gear, modelling spiked hair with Vim highlights. . . Now that fucking burned. Keith's outfit consisting of 26" high waisters tapered with bicycle clips, a General Lee, Dukes of Hazzard belt, his dad's old dinner jacket with skull bootlace, oh, and my borrowed red brothel creepers. . . all finished off with mirror glasses. I was in turquoise mohair with matching earrings; black bondage trousers adorned with numerous chains and safety pins and red plastic sandals. Real cool cats or in retrospect, real school twats.

Keith twitched into the club full of it, or as full of it that someone resembling a help the aged shop window could be, with me shuffling behind like Sid Vicious holding a shit in.

After hiding in the corner for an hour as blokes did, well actually we were still kids, I told Keith to remove his bicycle clips as his trousers had turned into plus fours. While he was busy folding his flares into his socks and checking his quiff, I strolled up to the DJ and requested a song as I couldn't stomach doing the British hustle again, and I definitely wasn't in the mood for dancing with Tina Charles.

"This one's going out to Simon and Keith from Luton. . . Not my cup of tea," said phoney Blackburn, but then The Stranglers "Go Buddy Go" twanged up, startling the cast from

Chain Saw Massacre on the first table. I immediately went pogoing onto the clearing floor in full Masai tribesman mode; Keith rode his imaginary space hopper and head butted the disco ball like an out of control clockwork toy. . . Anarchy on the dance floor. The punters where dumbstruck and after 40 seconds the owner came in doing a fair impression of the farmer in *Carry On Camping*.

"Stop that, no, no we can't have that in here, we're a respectable family club." The DJ apologised, and Dr Hook restored public order. We were then pulled to one side by two big fucking carrot crunchers probably named the Fison brothers. "Ere yous two townies behave or we'll break yewer fucking moosh right?"

We regrouped by the fruit machine. Keith said, "Let's go before we get a kicking, fucking inbreds."

I replied with a general reference containing bollocks and told him to look at those two birds in the corner. I really fancied the one in spandex with the big bazookas. I gave her a little wave; Keith checked out her frumpy mate wearing a Marc Bolan T-shirt with bib and brace.

"How come I always get the dumper truck?" He complained.

"We ain't got either yet coz we ain't even talked to them," I said in a whiny voice.

We drew cigar butts, and Keith lost, but to his credit, off he strutted to the beat of the strobe light with collar up and sunglasses on and fell straight into the girl's table like in a Buster Keaton movie.

Despite his disastrous entrance, within five minutes Miss

T-Rex or should I say Miss Trex wobbled up and led him to the centre of the dance floor. I noticed the yokels were still screwing us intently. The thought "fuck, I hope these two aren't property of the Wurzels" crossed my mind. I downed my Tolly Cobbold and bowled over to ask the bird with a chest full of puppies for a smooch.

"What's your name then?" She asked.

"Er, er it's umm Steve," I said. Not sure why.

"I'm Emma, where you from Steve?"

"errr I'm, we're from London."

"The DJ said you were from Luton?"

Time to play one's joker, I thought, so changing the subject I swung her round to face the two giants from it's a knockout.

"Do you know those two carrot crunchers?"

"No. We're not from round here; we're from Boston."

In shock, and great at geography, I stopped the dance and thought "Blimey, she's a septic."

"Did you come here with Freddy Laker?" I enthusiastically enquired.

"Who's he? No, with my friend Pauline and my aunty."

We took up the dance again. I inhaled on my cafe creme and while exhaling, said through the smoke in my best Clint Eastwood "Hey Emma, are you laughing at my mule?"

"Oh, I love John Wayne," she replied.

"Yeah, same hat," I said in disappointment.

Just then Hot Chocolate were suddenly faded out as the DJ said "It's raffle time folks." The lights went up, and Blackburn began "On the blue ticket. . ." I looked for Keith, and he was already tonguing Hattie Jacques junior. I couldn't believe it. Fumbling for change I asked Emma if she'd like a drink.

"Yeah tar, I'll have a Babycham."

"Would you like a cherry?" I said, showing off.

She said no, just stick a brandy in it. Fuck me, I only had a quid. I reckon she was about 18, maybe 18 and a half. I liked the older woman, well at 16, anything really. I left her my Toffos and strolled to the bar.

"Brandy and Babycham and a pint of Skol please."

I searched my pockets and found the quid plus two pence, a stick of Wrigleys and a Johnny. "This could be the night." I thought, checking the use-by date.

The barman, who was probably named Elvis, yet another sad seventies clone, said, "Well it's a one for the money. . . ."

Naa. Actually he snapped "Where's your I.D. then boy?"

Bollocks, all week they hadn't asked us and now of all nights.

"Err its in the caravan mate," was all I could manage.

I waved Keith over and then a meeting took place by the bog. "What're we gonna do Keith?"

"Well I've got my provisional for me moped," he said, "maybe we could forge the date."

So, stealing a pencil from behind a butcher's ear, we went in the cubicle and changed the six to five, so it now read D.O.B. 11/03/1951. Keith went back to the bar. The girls had now been surrounded by the young farmers club and were looking a bit sheepish.

Elvis stared at Keith's licence then burst into laughter. Still doing the sums, he said "26? You ain't even got a hair on your face! Go on, sling it you toe-rags. Tomorrow it's Cresta and crisps."

He burst out laughing again and accompanying cackles, and farmyard noises broke out behind us, even sniggers from our newly betrothed. The doorman, Selwyn Froggit, gave the nod and the Wurzels moved in to aim a real Suffolk punch. They were joined by Gummage and Mr Crowman. *Staying Alive* was appropriately playing as we were chased out and up the slippery lane. We ran and ran until we could no longer hear the sound of revving muck spreaders. I felt so gutted and angry at Elvis that I wanted to go back and take his sideburns off with a potato peeler. Mind you, little did I know reprisal was just round the corner, his world was due to come to an abrupt end in August as "the king" fell off his blue suede shoes. Mine was just beginning.

No Fun to Stay at the YMCA

You'd think I would have had enough of caravans, but in 1979 eight of us headed down to the Dorset Riviera. Well, it was a place called Bashley to be precise, which is about eight miles from Bournemouth, in the New Forest. A couple of the boys had been there the year before and had got lucky with females. They also made friends with a few local lads who owned real cars.

We piled down on the National coach. I remember thinking how the fuck was I going to pay back the 90 pounds I had gone overdrawn (over three weeks wages). Because back in those days you could write a cheque then nip round to the cashpoint and pull out the same amount before the teller could shout 'stop thief.'

The night before we left we pooled all our money, laid it on the carpet and took a Polaroid of over 700 pounds. . . We had never seen so much money. Of course, it all ran out mid-week, and we had to ponce of other people and borrow food from the local Mace. You'd be surprised what you can fit up your arse. Punk was still raging, but Dave, Ray and I decided we were now New Wave. But Rob, a Damned hardened disciple, stayed true to anarchy. Then there was Gary; the pint-sized full blown Teddy boy, which left Martin the Mod in Sherman, loafers and Sta-prest, Kev with his Keegan perm and Gez, the man at C&A.

We packed a lot into that week, including visits to Bournemouth to see the Jam and The Secret Policemans' Ball, ending up with an eventful night in the YMCA. We also had partial success in the clubhouse disco with young ladies and in the day went adder spotting or played football. New friends were made or reacquainted, Including Malcolm, AKA crater face, who owned an immaculate two litre Capri, come mini bus. I bet Ford never realised you could fit nine alleged adults into a two door.

The first amusing event was when Gary unpacked his case to find his prize drapes had been replaced by women's girdles. He was horror-struck, we were hysterical. A taxi took him back to the bus station where a slimy sales rep luckily had discovered his suitcase contained Freddy Star's wardrobe and returned. A discreet swap was arranged in the shadows of the urinal in the style of a spy movie, and Gary returned. Talking of suitcases, Dave's unbelievably contained two gallons of Daddies sauce (in bottles). The discovery of which reignited the great HP vs Daddies debate. Kev's bag was full of hairspray and scaffold ties, Martin's; Men Only and Escort, Ray's; a parachute suit with "destroy" emblazoned across the back and a bottle of homemade radish wine. Gez, the clever one, had the complete works of Chaucer and a blueprint for a General Electric aeroplane engine. Me? Well, I had a load of new gear from the club book that I knew I could never pay back. Sorry mum.

In the afternoon, we played football on the grass by the pool. I don't recall the weather, but I do remember the water was so cold that there were a group of brass monkeys looking for a welder. At 3-1 down against a collection of northern lads, I was stung by a bee. As we were playing barefoot, this resulted in a mass stampede. Twenty lads legging it into the clubhouse as if Freddy Krueger had nicked the ball. I pulled the bee out of my foot and waited in vain for St John's ambulance. Later in the bar Dave's uncle, a jolly giant of a man named Laurie, in the midst of consuming his 10th pint for brunch generously offered to buy us all a drink and gave his nephew a tenner.

Dave, who had sat out the match due to his guts being of a delicate nature and to safeguard against further Daddies sauce leaks, had stuffed his pants full of toilet roll. He then drew the attention of the lunch time crowd when he made his way back from the bar wobbling like a blancmange leaving a trail of brown sauce flavoured Andrex. . . Free advertising, but not quite as cute as a Labrador puppy we all thought. On putting down the tray of lagers, his uncle asked if he was on a paper chase as he seemed to have dropped something. The cleaner's Hoover was a write-off.

On disco night we had obtained the services of Steve McGarrett, a local boy of about 14 who wore a blue Hawaiian shirt, he was a good looking kid, looked a bit like the ill-fated River Phoenix although of course he was yet to be invented, and all the girls thought he was cute. We sent him on errands, especially ones to chat up birds before we moved in, thus avoiding total rejection. I remember Ray pulled a stunner called Kerry. This was not unusual as he had a bit of an English version of John Travolta about him. I ended up with a girl called Caroline, a six out of ten. As I looked up, most of the lads were too pissed to even care as Dave did the waltz in double time with his aunty to Sparks' *Beat The Clock*.

Gez had got off with a black haired girl, I can't, remember her name, but he had tried to chat her up by explaining Bernoulli's Theorem of flight and telling hilarious stories about differential fluid dynamics. Luckily it turned out she was mates with Caroline so after a quick discussion we retired with old English cider in hand to their caravan. We decided to swap girls, not as a plan, but because we just clicked better. Caroline was a student nurse, and Gez claimed to have read the Lancet. The other one washed hair in a cheap salon, so I showed her my head and shoulders and later my knob, which was when it went tits up. I couldn't work a front loader and had whispered to Gez to see if he had knowledge of the workings of bras. He started reeling off an instruction manual from Playtex. I got fed up by around item 13, subsection 4 and decided to just go for it. She had beef curtains like a baby stingray that almost put me off, but as I started to skin up, she said "no." I said "yes," she said "noo," I said "please," she said "no-wa," I said "I love you," she said "NOOOOOO." I said, "Well, fuck off then."

The next day crater face and his mate John turned up, and we all decided to go to Bournemouth.

John said, "Listen, boys we'll never fit all in one car, I'll go get my Austin 1100. . ."

"No thanks John, we'll fit in somehow," Ray said.

After all, who wanted to be seen in that maroon heap when we had a 2000GT Capri to pose in. To Malcolm's displeasure we all piled in, it was like being in a tin of jelly babies, Gez decided to get out and join John. This meant (pre-Guns n' Roses) the axle rose two inches from the floor, and we set off on a 20-minute ride that can only be compared to the horrors Bulgarian cattle endure during transportation. We crawled out of the vehicle and onto the sea front like zombies from the grave. Onlookers stood staring in disbelief.

"Right," we spoke in one voice. "Let's get in the first pub,"

It was called the Palace Vaults, and we decided a round of swamp water was called for. This was a 1970's version of Jägermeister and Red Bull, consisting of lager, cider and creme de menthe. It tasted like Colgate but got you lashed. In the afternoon, we rolled into the cinema and then rolled with laughter like the clown on the pier at the Secret Policemans' Ball with Rowan Atkinson, etc.

That night we went to see The Jam. They were great. The night ended in disarray when we got in a free for all with a load of grebo's (wanna be hell's angels) who where waiting outside to attack the punks. We just happened to come out as they came in. In the ensuing melee, we got split up and after giving a good account of ourselves, legged it into town. The four of us limped the streets with only about a quid between us.

"What are we going to do?" Asked Rob.

"Hitch a lift," replied Dave.

I pointed out that we looked like we'd been in a car crash and that we didn't even know the name of where we were staying. Just then Ray looked up and pointed. There, lit up in the night sky was a YMCA sign. We all shouted 'yes' in the manner of just having scored the cup final winner.

We gave the bloke at reception a cock and bull story that we had been set on and were down from London and missed the last train. He sympathised and led us up to a dormitory. As he gave the international sign for silence by pressing his finger to his lips, we passed the snoring village people.

"These are your four beds lads, sleep well."

"Cheers Eric."

They were all in a row; just like the three bears plus one.

"Who's gonna be Goldilocks?" I asked.

"You can have my porridge," offered Ray.

We clambered into bed, too tired and hungover to even wash. I don't remember anything else until I was woken by Rob's voice.

"Oi, fuck off. What're you doing mate?"

A man was trying to climb into Rob's bed. The whole dormitory was woken up by the man shouting "You're in my bed, get out of my bed you bastard."

The lights went on, Catweasle was half lying across Rob, who forcibly tossed him back onto the floor. Being a compassionate soul, aware of the plight of the homeless, Rob jumped out of bed and shouted, "Fuck off, you gypo."

The man lurched back and swung a haymaker at Ray, who blocked it, and, in another selfless charitable act, grabbed his beard and nutted him. "Oh no, here we go again," I thought.

The guy at reception, Eric, rushed in to separate them, followed by a wicked witch who was screaming "Leave Terry alone, that's his fucking bed."

By now a crowd had gathered, menacing looking pyjama clad hobos where moving in on us with fists clenched, being egged on by the female with the pointy hat.

We slowly backed up against the wall surrounded by the lady and the tramps. Eric said he was calling the police as two more workers ran into the dorm. More arguing ensued and scuffles broke out. Dave got slippered in the bollocks, but I knocked over Steptoe with a lucky shot. The police arrived.

"Right you lot, what's going on here then?" Said the sergeant, sticking to the script.

Fuck me, we were in the Secret Policemans' Ball again. Order was quickly restored, and the copper announced that any more trouble from anyone would result in them being knicked and then asked if we understood.

Catweasle continued to remonstrate and was led away by Dixon of Dock Green to be deloused. The cursing old hag was boiled in oil. The sergeant said to the gathered YMCA staff "God knows what's in the air tonight, we've been really stretched. . . A major disturbance had broken out at the Winter Gardens after a punk concert, so far we've made 17 arrests and rising."

We looked down at the floor again and innocently whistled.

The old bill left, and we sat on our beds while the enemy trudged back into their pits. It was now five am and dawn was arriving, so we decided to leave. On our way out we whistled "Gypsies, Tramps and Thieves," and consequently received a tirade of abuse, with shoes and plastic cups following us out of the swinging doors. We found a cafe and ordered four cups of tea and three rounds of toast, the cost of which was almost the total of our combined available funds. Dave rang Malcolm on a pay phone with the rest but there was no answer, and Dave surmised that it was far too early.

With our last 2p, we then rang a local taxi number that was on a card on the wall. The taxi driver said he knew where the site was. We arrived as the sun rose and swaggered onto the turf feeling like warriors returning from the movie with the same name but were soon put in our place by Dave's uncle, who had to fork out another tenner for the taxi. His sage-like advice for the rest of our stay at the seaside remains with me to this day.

"Stick to building fucking sandcastles."

The Rain in Spain

It's 1980. A new decade and the year Luton missed promotion by four points to Div 1. Incidentally, it was also the year Trevor McDoughnut told us of John Lennon's assassination, the failed U. S. hostage rescue attempt in Tehran, and the Mount St. Helen's eruption. The thing of course that Trevor forgot to mention was the lads' conquest of Benidorm.

Eighteen of us descended on the Costa Blanca, not quite Pontinental style but still Europe's most popular knock-kneed knackered resort. In summertime reserved for lager, lager, lager and in winter the invasion of the bingo bonkers walking dead. I could go on, but it has been well documented. Let's just say Benidorm is about as Spanish as Manuel from Farty Towels, sorry, Fawlty Towers. Although in its defence, the old town, El Castell, still retains its charm.

We arrived in a downpour, the rain in Spain did indeed fall mainly on our plane. Our hotel, the Castilla, was a typical cement monstrosity, serving Sam and Ella, Flamenco and heavy duty cocktails to Britain's finest tourists. While we were there a legionnaire outbreak occurred. . . The disease that is, not a French soldier prison escape. Our nights were filled with wine, women and song, i.e., bars, snogging and football anthems. Our days were filled with recovering round the pool with sporadic outbreaks of the Battle of Britain. I find it incredible we fought and won two world wars only to lose our sun beds.

Souvenir shopping was normally reserved for the last day with phrase book in hand. Straw donkeys, miniature barrels of brandy 103, Spanish dolls and Spanish fly-bulged from the squadrons of 1-11's returning the bronzed hoards home.

Three memories jump out at me, the first being see no evil, speak no evil, second the infamous Spanish barbeque night and last, but not least, D.I.S.C.O.

Speak No Evil

Slumped around the pool enjoying a lazy day of Milk of Magnesia Martini cocktails, the peace of the hazy afternoon was shattered when one of those imbecilic animal carrying photographers dumped a chimp onto our Dave's stomach. The shock of waking with a PG tips advert grabbing at his Percy Dalton's propelled Dave and the monkey into the deep end, scuppering big Sharon's airbed in the process. Within seconds the photographer was screaming, Sharon was submerging, the Chimp was screeching, and Dave was seething.

It was so funny I had to attach my snorkel to breathe. Luckily, Ramon the head barman and several waiters came to the rescue, with Latin diplomacy further heated arguments ensued, but eventually compensation was awarded, and all ended well when Sharon sang I'm forever blowing bubbles, that's West Ham, not the Chimp.

B.B.Q.

The next day was mainly spent on the beach; we returned to the hotel mid afternoon as ogling topless women loses its appeal after a while, plus the sun was doing its best to turn us into a Sunday roast. We all basted in shower gel and met in the foyer waiting for the coach at 6 pm. Presuming our destination must be far away, as six seemed early. The rain in Spain fell again. The bus arrived, incidentally the driver's name was Jesus, so I hid my straw donkey in case the rep was called Mary. The coach seemed to pick up from every hotel in the resort and by the time we got to Eldorado, about 10k from Benidorm it was 8 pm but at least the sun went down with its Cordobas on.

We all sat at a long table waiting for Jesus, who had our

food tickets, so we ordered several San Miguel's. While we waited, we discussed who would grass him up. At last he turned up; thank God for that. Then the grub was up. Bowls of salad drenched in Coppertone, boiled spuds in jackets, and apple fed pinky and perky were laid out evenly on the table. Endless jugs of cheap vino kept coming, so I kept drinking. During the feast, the ugly bloke from the good and the bad poured copious amounts of vinegar from a porron (skinny necked bottle) down our throats (and all down our shirts), all very amusing when you're eighteen and in Spain for the first time with your best buddies.

A mock bull fight was then staged. The bull was so tiny it looked more like a black labrador wearing a Viking hat. Ole, ole, oh fucking lay. Next the flamingo dancing and a chorus of Viva Espana, yeah, we All had a go. Then the grand finale, some awfully cheesy bloke called Sleepy Le Beef (the Señorita greeter) with Axminster chest, Mr. T's bling, Tom Jones packet and rose in teeth, gave his best renditions of Tony Christie's sherry song *Is this to way to Amontillado*. That got the juices flowing for the over 40's from Billericay.

By now I was absolutely legless. I remember staring at a real donkey called Medusa who had seven heads. Next thing I'm being woken up am, time and dragged out of a cactus bush into a taxi. Apparently some of us had missed the coach. Dave said the driver couldn't wait any longer and had to go, or his boss would crucify him. So off we travelled in Noddy's car, a red Seat 500, down the mountain Italian Job style. After three bends, my stomach moved into my mouth.

"Let me out," I slurred "Let me out, I'm gonna spew."

I then pulled the window handle off and forced the window down, hanging out of the car like a big dog and was then sick like him for 4 kilometres. I know it was four kilometres because the next day we hired motorbikes and went back to measure it and photograph my new world record. To this day, I still blame the IRA for not getting my record in Guinness.

D.I.S.C.O.

We entered the Black Sabad disco on the advice of the free ticket wielding scouser outside. "It's grayte in dare mate, lowds of fanny and good sounds and only 300 potatoes."

"OK mate, lads, let's do it."

Fourteen of us entered an empty club. Lying fucker.

We ordered a ridiculous amount of drinks as per usual. Dave decided to down half a pint of Bacardi, which came straight back out of his mouth and into his glass. He turned to Steve and asked if he wanted to try his pina colada.

"Cheers," said Steve, who got a third of the way down then refilled the glass again with a fruit salad.

"You dirty bastard, Dave." Laughter broke out about the same time as a fight when HMS Newcastle spilled through the door. The barmen rushed them, and the scuffle continued outside.

In a flash we were up over the bar, passing bottles back in a line like professional wreckers when someone remarked that it was free. 300 pesetas all you can drink. Errr not enough knotted handkerchiefs to keep off the sun perhaps? We passed them all back behind the bar and then tried to convince each other we were decent lads, and we would have paid for them anyway.

After about an hour, the club started to fill up. There were Brits, Germans and some Dutch and a few Norwegians. Then five Swedish birds glided by. Absolute stunners. We all let out howls of approval and thought about the usual questions. "Do you drive a Volvo, do you know the dancing queen, do you do Swedish massage, Wanna see my meatballs?" Naaaa all too naff, even for young Turds like us.

We sent Ray over as he had borrowed Brian Ferry's haircut for the holiday. He came back defeated in under five minutes. Fucking hell, we've got no chance then.

"What did they say, Ray, what did they say?"

"Errr I opened with love is the drug then told them the joke about the turnip and the Swede."

"You are fucking joking?" Said Royston.

"Well, I don't know any Swedish."

"Don't they speak English then?" Asked Steve.

"I think so," said Ray. "But look, they're after older blokes with sharks teeth round their necks, who shave and chew shag, not gimps with cheap St Christopher's who want one."

"It's called snus." Said, Robby.

"I prefer shag," I said.

We then cried in resignation as a group of handsome white uniformed American sailors moved in. Fucking Osmonds. As the night progressed, we were collectively rejected more times than Capone from the parole board. So at about twoish we left defeated and on the way home split up.

As Ray and I stumbled through the lanes complaining about the endless noise pollution as Spain was in the grip of the soundtrack to Grease, as opposed to the soundtrack to Greece, which was mainly Nana Mouskouri, we came upon three young maidens from Maidenhead.

"Where you going darling?" Never fails that one. Giggles. They were more pissed than us.

"We're going where you're going boys," said the blonde one.

Result, get in there.

After a quick rendition of the first three bars of Match Of the Day, we sobered up instantly. Their cheap perfume was like snorting a line of smelling salts.

"Right then, what're your names girls? Where yous from?"

"We're from all over; we're in the Navy."

So with arms interlinked we marched off up the hill singing the Grand of Duke of York he had 10,000 wrens.

As we approached reception to our TT hotel, we were stopped by Ballesteros, the security guard.

"Sorry, amigos, no girl in the room."

Exactly, that's why we're bringing them in," I joked.

You comprendo, NO girl in ROOM."

"You are joking? Look here's 200 potatoes practice your chipping."

"You no listen, see now you fuck English, no girl go room, or I call Carabineros."

Just our luck to get a fascist left over from Franco's army. One of the girls called him a very bad man and he replied that she was a prostitute.

"Steady on mate," said Ray.

We turned and walked away, the girls shouting their best abuse that included timeless classics like "Dago bastard wop, go fuck offo" and other colourful Iberian insults.

They then led us back to their hotel, a larger communist block. During the early morning, I woke up in strange surroundings and slid out of bed looking for the toilet. I felt like shit and had one. I was elated I'd scored. Goooooooooooooooooooooal with petty officer Debbie, a holiday shag. Ray was in the next room with the other two, but that was OK, the girls said he was more Travolta than Ferry and all agreed 'He's the One that I want.'

When we got back to our hotel in the morning around 7 am, we discovered Dave, semi-nude, crouched by the tennis courts. He explained that apparently he had pulled a female version of Archie Gemmel in the Rangers' bar and in the middle of the night while going for a piss, got lost and walked into the wrong room.

After getting into bed with a middle-aged German couple, everyone concerned freaked out, and the man chased the near naked Dave with a big cock bottle opener down the corridor. Luckily, Dave had his pants and socks on, and he escaped down the fire exit. Dave spent a lot of the morning dodging from palm tree to palm tree on his toes looney toon style. We went up to his balcony and got him some union jack shorts. He fell asleep on a lounger. Not a monkey or German in sight.

CHAPTER 4

Vait a Minute, Pleaze

"It's here," mum shouted. I galloped my hobby horse down the stairs and into the kitchen and there on the table was a letter with those magic words emblazoned across the top in blue: Barclaycard Visa. Our ageing dog's eyes nervously followed all the commotion, then with fiendish face and guarded look, I clasped it Fagin-style to my chest and then hurried into the toilet locking Rex out and displacing several displeased cats warming on the boiler. Prizing the letter open, now with bulging eyes like Gollum I got my first look at my precious. Not quite the power of the ring, but close.

It slipped itself into my wallet and snuggled down with the cigarette coupons and taxi cards, so I slipped it under the cellophane pocket to give it pride of place. What was my credit limit? Feverishly I ran my eyes over the letter again. Wow, £600 that was mega, in 1980 about seven times my weekly wage, I told my mum it was only 200 pounds. Dad said "Don't go nuts, remember you have to pay it back,"

"Yeah, yeah whatever."

I closed the front door and punched the air, then jumped on to the No. 28 bus and went straight up to my local to show my mates. I was like a kid who'd found the golden ticket for Willy Wonka's.

The next day I arranged a meeting with Dave downtown, outside Wimpy's we bumped into Chubb, a fellow drinker at our local, the Royal Oak. Somehow he latched on to us as we then made a b-line for Lunn Polly, the travel agent. After sifting through the usual destinations that were way too expensive even for my precious, the agent, who looked like Barry Gibb, asked if we had thought about a train journey.

"Do they go to Shanghai?" I asked sarcastically.

"No mate, through Europe" he replied with a tut then informed us he had done it last year, and it was brilliant.

Chubb commented, "I ain't going to no Shanghai, they eat dogs."

Dave asked him what he thought was in a pancake roll, and added "Who said you're coming anyway?" We studied the routes and came up with London-Paris-Basel-Zürich-Interlaken.

I asked Dave if he thought Rob would be in for it and he

thought it would be a yes. So I booked three tickets. Chubb was gutted, when the agent told him that Transalpino tickets are for the under 25's only. Chubb had been 26 for the last fifteen years.

Next stop Millets. We approached the sales manager looking up from his paperwork.

"Yeees?" He said. Count Dracula style, "Can I help you, laddie?"

"Yeah mate, have you got any two man tents that can fit four?"

"No, but we have four man tents that can fit two."

"Yeah, nice one. Look we're off to Switzerland, so we need err. . . besides the tent, some pots, Kendal mint cake and an ice axe. . ."

"Oh. And a compass," said Dave.

"Well laddie, as it's September, I think you may only need the tent and some sleeping bags."

Ian Drury's Clever Trevor sprung to mind. We ended up with an orange two man tent made from anti-yeti proof material, a cow bell and three army green sleeping bags endorsed by the homeless.

"OK, I need a rucksack now to carry it in," I said.

"Oh, you mean a Bergan laddie, the correct term is Bergan."

This bloke is a more of a fruit bat than a vampire, I thought.

"Listen Count," I said, "I don't give a toss what its name is and stop calling me laddie, grand-daddy. Do you want this sale or not?"

His smirk disappeared as Dave showed him his crucifix.

"That will be £46.20p, lad. . . er, please."

"You do realise that Switzerland is the most expensive country in the world?" Said Rob's mum, adding, "and don't forget your flask."

"Mum, I'm 20 years old."

It was like a sketch from the Vicks Synex ad with Malcolm and his mum.

"I'm still your mother," she replied.

"Where have I heard that before?" I thought.

She grabbed Rob and assumed the position with licked hankie in hand to wipe his face. He pulled himself away like the cat from Pepe la-pew and managed to bundle himself and his giant suitcase out of the front door.

"Send me a postcard," called his mum.

Rob thought this request would be expensive to comply with.

I had my Bergen on, which was heavier than I'd imagined. Dave had an Admiral Man Utd bag in one hand a cow bell round his neck and the compass in the other hand and informed us that the train station was north by north-west. Rob asked him if he was Cary Grant.

"Who?" We both replied.

"Some old movie bloke my mum likes."

"Does Mr. Squirrel know?" I asked, referring to the flirting odd job man who had a gigantic gusset and frequently visited Rob's mum to trim the grass with nail clippers.

"Naaaa, his truss exploded. . . forget it anyway. Let's go."

We boarded the 10 am train to St Pancras then onto Waterloo by tube and down to the coast onto the ferry that connected with the SNCF train to Paris Gare du Nord, where we spent a day looking for Rob's sister near Pigalle, where else? We took a picture of the Moulin Rouge and then jumped on the metro and took more pictures of the Eiffel Tower and Notre Dame on our cheap Kodaks, just to prove we had been there. After a swift few Kronenbourgs, we headed back to Gare du Nord where a train took us to Gare de Lyon where we boarded the night train to Switzerland, pretty secret service for those days.

We had our own little carriage and soon made ourselves at home scoffing down pretzel crackers, and Comte cheese all washed down with cheapo bouteilles de vin rouge. Although in Paris we had dumped our bags in left luggage, Rob's arms had grown three inches with the strain of dragging his treasure chest around, so he decided to repatriate it by chucking it out of the door just past Strasbourg, killing two cows and a stripy onion seller in the process. At about five am, we were woken by a Henri De Toulouse-Lautrec lookalike tapping the wheels with a hammer. Dave, ever the international diplomat, shouted out the window.

"Oi mate, we're trying to sleep here. Can't you use a rubber one?"

"Vait a minute pleaze." Came the reply.

A phrase we were to use over and over again on our trip. We arrived in Basel blurry eyed about 10 am. It was very foggy.

A disappointed Rob said, "Oh, I wanted to see the mountains."

As we waited to change trains the mist cleared, and we found the only mountains on view, were made of coal in a siding. Next stop the great city of Zurich, home to 200000 insurance workers. We dumped our bags again at the station and went to explore. We only managed 50 metres before we had to stop at a cafe and gorge ourselves with their amazing cakes. We sipped strange coffee called espresso from doll's house cups and gulped on ale filled vases from the planet Vulcan. . . Not a pork pie or Light 'n Bitter in sight.

The next day we set off for Interlaken, a town in the centre of the mountainous Jungfrau region that includes the famous Eiger. We played cards on the train and lost all our money to Dave along with IOU's.

The scenery was breathtaking, as the mountains grew bigger and bigger the weather closed in, and the ranges seemed to be in thunderous conflict. The crags and summits were scattered throughout the sky. Obviously I'm not a poet, but you get the picture.

On arriving at Interlaken, our first job was to purchase a rucksack for Rob, as his Spar bags were splitting at the seams.

We found a plush shopping centre and a sports shop. Rob liked the look of a Grasshoppers holder, that's a Swiss football team, not an insect jar, but he didn't like the price so much. He eventually settled for a black haversack that did the job. I decided I needed to drop the kids off, so I found the toilets. I entered through the archway and thought blimey, it was like a palace compared to the bogs in the Arndale Centre. I closed the cubicle, but it wouldn't lock.

Then there was a knock. I peered round the door like Kenneth Williams to see a former Olympic hammer thrower dressed in a white coat with matching bouffant towering in front off me.

"Gib mir bitte einer Franken," she ordered.

"Err sorry, do you speak English Fraulein?"

"YOU IN KLOSSET ME EINER FRANC," she said loudly, with arms folded.

"Oh, money, you want money?"

"Ja, einer franc."

I dug deep and offered my outstretched hand. "Nine? You said one! Nine, I haven't got nine, that's expensive for a shit."

Her face grew taut and serious. "Give me Swiss franc. Nein, no Frankreich franc."

She then pulled one franc from her bag and showed me.

"Oh yea, yea, sorry, excuser housen."

Rats, I haven't got any Swiss money left. . . and in my best German. "Iche go wezel change franc OK bitter?"

She laughed, smiled and then closed and locked my door. My urge to go waned as the kids had climbed back into the bomb chamber, but I managed a small Messerschmitt; after all 35p is a pint in Luton. Another knock on the door. "Beeilen (hurry up)."

"OK, OK". I pulled the handle, and she unlocked the door and pointed to her watch while still wanting two Francs. On reaching outside Rob duly obliged

"Let's find a room with a view for tonight," said Rob.

So we checked three small hotel tariffs. The prices were absolutely extortionate, so we bought a map that had lots of campsite signs on it and decided to head up the nearest mountain. We took a local train to base camp and trudged up a one-in-two hill for an hour. Finally arriving in a small lane that had a homemade sign with a tent and arrow indicating straight on 50 metres, we waited another half an hour for Dave, who was a large boy, to clamber up. He arrived breathless.

"Where's the fucking cable car?"

"Come on Bunter."

As we surveyed the valley and the lakes below Rob said, "just smell that air."

"Yea," said Dave as he lit up a fag.

For a small amount of shrapnel, we booked five nights at the camp and decided to pitch the tent next to the flowing stream and set off to explore. The site was about the size of a bumpy football pitch with a Wimbledon slope and the occasional pine tree plus mini-orchard that had covered the grass in windfall apples. We had great fun crunching around.

After even more fun re-erecting our tent, which had already collapsed, we then visited the farm shop and purchased six litres of white wine and ten packs of milk biscuits, Lays and Suchard for a minor amount. Hey, who said Switzerland was expensive? This is great, the great outdoors. I felt like a song "The hills are alive, with the sound of moo, ding dang, A giant purple cow shit the life out of me he was standing behind me licking at my elbow.

"Help, help."

The lads ran off, then out of the shop, help came in the shape of Herr Macdonald.

"Vot is ze truble, boy?"

"I'm being attacked by Ermintrude from the Magic Roundabout," I said in jest.

"Don't you haf ze cowz in England?" He asked.

"Yeah but not in our houses."

The others grabbed me round the head, and we set off down the lane passing strange gingerbread houses and small restaurants made from Alpen boxes. On our return, we had a pleasant surprise. Two English girls had pitched up next to ours. Rosie and Cilla seemed friendly enough, and as we sat and drunk Eidelweiss Blanc, they told us about their adventures backpacking across Europe. I don't know why but I sensed it was leading up to something.

After the third litre, Dave was getting on so well with Cilla he offered her the chance to come inside love. They were from Birkenhead, in their early twenties, slightly porky, one blond and one brunette. After two hours, we had exhausted all our Scouser jokes, and they had replied with their Chas 'n Dave routine, although Luton is 30 odd miles from the East end. Anyway, Rosie then starts with the crocodile tears.

"What's up darling," asks Dave.

"I was raped in Italy," she explains, "And they stole all our money. "Could you lend us a few pounds to get home?" She sobs.

A poor attempt at a play for today and a hundred percent crocodile tears.

I glanced at the boys and said "Case proved yer honour". . "Vait a minute, pleaze."

We decided to have a lads conference while purchasing more wine. The farmers wife in full kit was very voluptuous and had a full set of milkers. We stood frozen like the cast from Watership Down on the M25 and decided she was a Swiss/German mature porn star. I invited her to join me at ten for a cup of hot Lindt, and I promised to keep my socks on. She smiled and remarked on our new neighbours. Yes, nice girls from England.

"No, they're from Liverpool," said Rob.

She looked puzzled; we paid and as we walked back we all agreed we were lending them fuck-all.

We sat down. "Look, girls," said Rob, "We feel sorry for you and all that, but you should go to the police or the British embassy and here's our cowbell in case you get any more trouble."

Cilla flipped and spewed a tirade of abuse from her fat gob as we sat in stunned silence. Rosie accused us of being heartless typical cockneys; then they got up staggered back to their tent. We decided to call it a night as we were pretty slaughtered. Everybody knows three into two don't go, and although Rob was little, Dave was large (but funnier). It still added up to three. After half an hour, we managed to squeeze into our sleeping bags and settle down. Then ping, ping, the tent pegs were trying to escape. We couldn't be arsed and just crashed out as our tent crashed in.

A lone rooster sounded the alarm at about six. I struggled to open my eyes; then a fierce pain from my arse matched my head. I turned to see Dave stabbing at me with a Swiss army knife.

"What the fuck are you doing?" I shouted.

"Don't move, there's a tarantula on your bum." He replied.

Rob sat up and informed him that you don't get tarantulas as this is Switzerland not Swaziland. We all jumped up, and sack raced away from our wreckage. Dave laughingly apologised and said he was only doing what he'd been taught in Sunday school. But I was still fuming. I took my frustration out by pelting the girl's tent with mushy apples. Then the boys joined in, and we gave the tent a medieval stoning. We must have fired over 200 Bramleys. "They shouldn't need to visit the doctor for a year." I thought.

Interlaken sits slightly elevated on the Aare River and between two lakes, Thon and Brienz; It was a roasting day well into the 80's (old money), so we decided to take a leisurely boat trip around Lake Brienz. On reaching the Staubbach Falls, we alighted and decided to climb the falls for a better look. We got many a curious look from the swarms of hikers who filled the trails; all kitted out with Chris Bonnington's new summer collection. As for us big boots, cut downs and knotted hand-kerchiefs. After all only Englishmen with clogs go out in the mid-day sun. As we climbed, the path became more and more precarious until we came across an old rickety railway bridge spanning a very deep crevasse. We clung onto one another like refugees as we inched across the old wooden sleepers, which then deteriorated to crawling on hands and knees.

The drop must have been over 200 feet. The bridge creaked and swayed as we came to a petrified halt. Now laying flat on the floor, Dave said that we needed to turn back, it's not going to hold us. Rob disagreed and reckoned we must carry on. I told them to stay where they were and volunteered to go and get help. Just then, the Swiss family Robinson breezed past, wished us a Gooden Morgen and briskly marched on as if they were going for a Sunday stroll, not crossing the most frightening bridge in the world. Feeling like tossers, we sat up nervously laughing and after wishing them a good morning asked them to call International Rescue. Not understanding, they smiled and waved. We sat there for a further minute not talking.

"Right," I said, "If they can do it, so can we. Two world wars and one world cup chaps."

"They're Swiss, not Nazis." Said Rob.

"Yes, but they still have all their stolen art."

"OK then, in the spirit of the Great Escape."

"Bagsy I'm Steve McQueen," said Dave.

We held hands like we were taking a curtain call and sprinted back with eyes half closed until we reached the safety of the path. Then we fell on the floor hysterically laughing like Norman Wisdom. Oh Mr. Grimsdale, oh, Mr Grindlewald, Oh Mr. fucking hell, we repeated over and over until Virgil touched down in Thunderbird 2.

The next day we took a leaf out of Julie Andrews' songbook and climbed every mountain. Dave got his arse out on the top the mountain, Eye of the Eiger, but later that night we did make arseholes of ourselves while dining in a Michelin two-star joint in the picturesque village of Murren, which is situated below Shilthorn mountain. This was the mountain they used in James Bond's On Her Majesty's Secret Service with George Lazyass.

"OK lads, last night. I reckon I got about 80 sovs left on the card so let's have a feast."

We reviewed the menu; the prices were steeper than the mountain, so we ordered French fries for six, four omelettes with cheese slices, salad and three bottles of house wine plus the obligatory beer of course. That would total around 70 quid, I had reckoned, leaving £10 for the service charge.

The waiter approached and looked down his nose. It was longer than the ski runs. He soon delivered four bowls of soup.

"Er, excuse me garcon, these are not ours," said Rob.

It is free sir, complimentary."

"Oh, top man, cheers Gibeson." (Bignose butcher's slang).

We ate everything, including the condiments and the plant pot, being as that we were starving and bored of muesli and chocolate. After the alcohol had kicked in, Dave decided to enter the kitchen and compliment the chef on his French fries. Luckily he took it in good humour and did his lap of the tables to check the other diners were satisfied.

Then we spotted him, in the corner. Who? It was only the actor who sang *Whispering Grass* in It Ain't Half Hot Mum. His eyes met ours, but he shied away as Rob bellowed "Alright lofty?"

He half waved, as his mate turned and twiddled his handlebar moustache, after a few more beers, it started. First Dave with a chorus of the theme tune to the program.

Then "Oi Lofty," from Rob, "Where's lardydar Gunner Graham?"

I stood up and did an impression of Windsor Davies with a "Right, now my lovely boy," but I sounded more Pakistani than Welsh. We called the waiter and ordered three more large ones and told him to bring Lofty and Prince Albert a beer. Lofty declined and stood up to go. Well, he stood down really as his high chair was just that. He nodded and shuffled out the door with his mate without even a "see-ya lads."

"What an arsehole," said Rob. In retrospect, it may have been us! The couple mounted a penny farthing and freewheeled into the night.

The bill arrived, and the waiter smiled. I smiled and laid my Visa card down on his tray.

"No, sorry."

"You what?"

"Nein."

"Don't fucking start that again."

"We don't take Visa here sir, have you American Express or Diners Club.?"

I checked my wallet just for show and said, "Sorry, left them in the tent."

The boys looked worried. "OK mate, vait a minute pleaze."

The bill totalled 310 Francs, which Dave reckoned was around 110 pounds. "Oh shit," we said in unison.

"Right," said Dave, "It's time for the Shite of India trick."

"You don't mean?" Said Rob.

"I do," said Dave.

We all broke for the door sending the next table and the von Trapps flying. The staff just stood like statues, obviously having never had this happen before.

We fell into the road and slid over the meadow faster than Franz Klammer. Covering three miles in 15 minutes, it was easy going downhill. We reached a farm and collapsed in a heap we had no idea where we were. I suggested we hide in the barn for a while like fugitives; It was agreed. Several dogs were barking, so we crept up into the hay loft where we thought we heard sirens, but it may have been Kojak on the farmer's TV.

The next morning we woke to pissing rain. The mountains were covered in pea soup. How were we going to get home? We started our route march down the lane in the pouring rain. Asking two or three yodellers the way to Vidervill we got no response. I said I wished I had kept my wayfinders. We then came across the cable car and hitched a lift down the valley to a place called Wegen, where we got a bus to Wildersville then onto Interlaken. Managing to dry off partly on the bus, we spent the afternoon sitting in a cafe with collars up and caps down. Every time we saw a police car we buried our heads in the Emmental Echo.

We spent our last night quietly reflecting on a great week. The journey home was tedious and tiring and by the time I got back to Luton my card was on its limit. The lads, of course, promised to help pay it back. But I knew it would be down to me. As I sat back in the local taxi, I reminisced and congratulated myself on having had three holidays that year. Weymouth, Benidorm and Switzerland with the lads. A good start to the decade.

When we stopped, the taxi driver said "Two pounds twenty chief."

Looking in my wallet, I replied "Vait a minute pleaze."

CHAPTER 5

Eurotrash

Harry Palmer likes Green Peppers

I had just passed through Checkpoint Charlie. Is that it? I thought, one of the most iconic cold war landmarks. I'd conjured up visions of walls of barbed wire and machine gun turrets with huge spot lights, not an NCP barrier and a few sand bags. Disappointed, I trundled off to find the remaining bit of wall.

As you may have gathered, I'm in Berlin, the re-badged capital of a Germany Utd. I wandered the city and let my imagination run riot as I goose-stepped under Brandenburg gate with the 5th Panzer division in an imaginary procession during the Third Reich, I then turned into Leipzig Strasse. In a split second, I was on the run, swallowing microfilm from my Minox as the Stasi black Mercedes screeched round the corner. The wall was a disappointment as most of it has been hacked down and sold off as souvenirs; some had been attached to postcards, so I decided to send my brother a little piece of history but for all I knew it could have been reproduced by Lego.

I took a stroll and checked out the watchtower, not a Jehovah witness in sight! It was positioned at the end of no man's land in the old East. I climbed and reached the observation point then I looked out and imagined Philby, Burgess and MacLean all crammed into a Trabant having their papers checked. There was an information point that read, amongst other things, that the East German police had one operative for every 166 people residing in the former DDR. With this in mind I reworked an old Elvis Costello song, pulled up my collar up and whistled watching by detectives until it was time for shopping.

After a random purchase of a Hertha football t-shirt and an I love Berlin Teddy. I found myself outside a small theatre/cinema that amazingly was showing *Funeral in Berlin* and *The Ipcress File* in a double header, too good to miss for a mere 5 euros. I purchased a ticket from Pinocchio in the Punch and Judy booth and slipped between the curtains. A wall sign with an arrow pointed upstairs to a pool hall said to be run by the guy from Boney M (r.i.p), but I proceeded down the 39 steps into the cinema. I loaded my Walther PPK and inconspicuously moved into the front row, and close enough to jump into the screen if needed.

Although a little cramped, the theatre was in good

condition. It was a sort of mish-mash of goth meets deco style with a strong smell of spiced lamb and Turkish coffee seeping in from next door. I wondered about its history and if maybe Adolf had sat in my seat with a stiffy perving over Marlene Dietrich all twanged up on stage until I saw a plaque on the wall stating this theatre was opened by Herr Hamburger in 1949. Luckily the film was in English with German subtitles and surprisingly it was pretty full, probably eighty odd people made up of a few tourists like me, a hardcore of Berliners, and the ghost of Anthony Blunt plus the local film critic Baron von Norman.

The screen flickered. Paramount Pictures presents an Otto Heller film it read. And off we went, after Funeral in Berlin finished, I stood up stretched and sent a morse code for refreshments, I purchased a mustard-smothered frankfurter and an Americano from coco the clown, no Kia-ora and Lyons Maid I'm afraid, and I half excepted an usher on stilts to appear and show me back to my seat, perhaps a circus had closed down. I settled back again spreading mustard all around my chops.

About half way through the Ipcress File we reached a scene where Michael Caine, as Harry Palmer is chopping up green peppers and showing off his culinary skills with a tin of champignons, obviously a luxury item back in 1965. He was trying to impress some bird, but she was having none of it, it was going to take more than mushrooms to get her in the sack. Unfazed, he his took his frustration out on six eggs. The virtual smell of his omelet made me hungry again; I checked my man from uncle watch It was 21.58 and 13 seconds so I left by the fire exit, as I knew by now it would be getting dark outside.

After strolling through two narrow streets, I was sure I was being followed, the sound of blakey-heeled brogues echoed behind me. I then noticed dozens of guys wearing macs who seemed to be watching me over their newspapers. Thinking I had let imagination and Harry Palmer run away with me, I gazed at a weasel faced man in a doorway who looked rather out of place, he should have been in Death on the Nile, not my Len Deighton story. He wore a tilted Panama and dirty cream safari suit with a plaster holding his thick rimmed glasses in place. He gazed back at me then took a long drag on his Lucky stripe and flicked it onto the floor. Flipping his Zippo shut, he stepped back into the shadows and was replaced by Midge Ure in white a Mac. Of course this meant nothing to me. Then it dawned on me they were not spies at all, but dirty old men in raincoats.

I was in a porn area. Get a grip man, I thought as I shook my head at my stupidity. Suddenly a faceless man took my smile away as he jabbed me in the leg with his umbrella. Fuck, done by the KGB.

I awoke in a dentist's chair.

"IS IT SAFE?" He repeatedly asked me.

"Errr yeah well safe geezer." I replied.

I awoke again in a sweat, but soon panic turned to relief as I was still in the cinema. I'd fallen asleep. I laughed out loud, which in those days didn't have an acronym. The man next to me turned and glared with disapproval as if to say what's funny about a bloke from MI6 getting his head stoved in? I slid back down in my chair like in the Mr. Bean sketch then frightened myself with a shadow of someone getting up behind me. I checked my leg, then my teeth, yep still there.

At the end of the Ipcress File, Harry Palmer is faced with a dilemma. He must choose between two supposed double agents who then try to double bluff him with their loyalties to the crown. Harry kills the correct one, a smatter of applause (common in continental cinemas) broke out. Cue music and lights. We filed out up the spindly staircase, the proprietor, unsurprisingly a Colonel Stock lookalike, grabbed my arm and invited me back next week for *Billion Dollar Brain*.

"Danka" I replied, clicked my loafers and strolled out into a pleasant summer's evening.

I decided to dine in a small street cafe and went for something very traditional. No, not Eisbien (pork knuckle) but a shish kebab accompanied by three pots of Holsten, absolutely tremendous. After people watching for an hour, I decided to head back to the hotel.

As I ambled along, I came across a wank booth; that is to say, a row of cubicles in a sex shop that are fed by coins showing old adult movies. I checked my change, four euros, sixty cents. "Well that's at least half an hours' worth of maggot thrashing," I thought as I fed the slot and closed the door behind me. I felt a shiver as the air con was set on freezing but fuck it, the four euros were in.

I flicked through dozens of movies; the choice was endless, but suddenly I wasn't in the mood for Deiter does Düsseldorf.

My mind drifted back to Amsterdam many moons ago when I had been in a similar position and was just on my vinegar stroke when the credit clock ran down and suddenly switched off, as did the lights. I quickly adjusted my attire in the blackness then gingerly crept out into the corridor only to be met by a cleaner who looked me up with a look of total disgust.

"Dirty Dirty," she snarled.

"No need for that Mrs," what does she think blokes are in here for, Van der Valk? Then I looked down, urrrr my shorts were covered in jizz.

Meanwhile back in Berlin the countdown on the screen had begun 8,7,6. . . Legen Sie mehr Geld. . . insert more dosh you wanker, flashed the screen… then pitch darkness.

"Oh for fuck's sake," I muttered.

Then with my best braille, I unlocked the door and smashed my nose as it didn't budge. Shit, I tried again but it wouldn't move, so I heaved and hoed but it was locked tight.

"OK, stay calm son." I said to myself.

The next plan was a reverse karate kid kick. . . Still nothing. Bollocks. I decided in a last resort to give it a Big Daddy shoulder barge; if it broke, so be it.

So with a six inch run-up, I crashed into the door and rebounded back and lumped my head on the wall. FUCK, I should have known you can't beat German efficiency. . . I calmed myself again then let out a small high pitched "Help."

Silence. Probably only heard by a passing dachshund I

thought, so I followed quickly with a distress call of help followed by I need somebody. Still nothing. I thought Germans liked the Beatles? Oh yeah, that was Hamburg. So I resorted to shouting "HEEEEEEEEELP" at the top of my voice.

"Please, I'm too young to die."

Not a whisper.

As I didn't have a flare or an oxyacetylene torch handy, panic started to set in. This was no dream; it was a nightmare. I was shivering by now and hyperventilating, the correct thing to do in here but for the wrong reason.

Was I to spend the night in Berlin trapped in a wank booth? Tune in next week folks for more escape from Coldtits. Suddenly, just as I saw strange lights and a welcoming tunnel, there was a ping and the door opened. I peered outside, taking a moment to recover, no one home. Duh, of course it must of been set on a time delay for zipping up and sleeve wiping and I despaired when I saw the light switch outside the booth. I hurried down the road like a shoplifter and mingled into the crowd with all the other wankers.

The next morning I made my way down to breakfast. Now I have stayed in some top class hotels but this one was just a small two star jobbie, however, the buffet breakfast could have fed the 5,000. Was Jesus working the kitchen this morning? The dining room was filled with tourists, mainly Germans from other parts, some in full lederhosen. I concealed my amusement by stuffing my face with fish and loaves and then, after a shower, I checked out and took myself to the airport for a short flight to Luton.

A word of warning; there are three airports in Berlin. Make sure you do your homework if you are changing flights.

Gorillas on the Piss

Berlin is now on the A list for stag nights, joining Hamburg and a host of other European cities like Amsterdam and Prague. Now the Baltic countries have cashed in, trebling their hospitality prices for soon-to-be grooms from Beerfordshire. Regarding myself, having been there and done it until it became tiresome, I think I have enough t-shirts to start a mail order company. Amsterdamage, which was almost my second home in the eighties, has many fond memories for me, but probably the funniest stories I have involved the Weise beer festival back in '85 and a trip to Ostend for the last man standing tour of '98.

Belgium, for some reason, has always been the butt of many a European joke. In fact, the country is still at unofficial civil war between the Flemish Dutch and the French speakers and they genuinely seem to not like each other. As a destination, if you take Brussels out of the equation, it has some great cities like Bruges which is a must see stunningly beautiful medieval city. If possible, get yourself, a copy of the movie *In Bruges* it's one of my favourite films. I highly recommend them both.

One of Belgium's many beer festivals is in Weiss. OK, it doesn't quite rival King Munich, but it's a hoot and with over 200 breweries flogging their wares even Oliver Reed would have struggled to do the card. The weekend was a blur, but I do have one sweet-bitter memory of being attacked by an extra from Planet of the Apes.

I had decided to take a break from boozing as it was only mid-afternoon, and I was starting to struggle as we had been on it since breakfast at 0700.

I wandered through the old fair to get some low country air and decided, for some alcohol-fueled reason, to queue up for the Hurricane Jets, an air ride with mini planes on hydraulic arms like you used to get in UK fairgrounds when I was a kid. In retrospect, this is not a great idea when your stomach contains two vats of Trappist's finest. I approached the small hut and handed over my 20 franc note through a small window. I quite fancied number two in a shiny British racing green.

Suddenly I was yanked forward against the glass; it was a full on catch the pigeon collision and stars soon appeared. Then for a split second my reflection became a monkey. As the mist cleared I realised, fuck me, I wasn't concussed, a psychotic chimpanzee had got hold of my arm. I tried to pull back but the fucker was super strong, his assistant Billy Smartarse grabbed the chimp and tried to make him let go pulling by tickling his armpit (yeah that'll work then) but he just got more irate and pulled a toothy grin. A tug of war then ensued between Jim Carrey and me, then suddenly he let go, and I was propelled backwards onto my arse.

I was absolutely fuming, so I stormed around the back of the booth, where me and the monkey swapped insults in Jabawocky for a while. I'll give you fucking Ooh ah ah. Several people tried to intervene, but then the resident strongman come Tarzan appeared and quickly got me in an headlock. These fuckers were working as a tag team, the chimp then landed a haymaker that almost broke my nose and not satisfied with this he then jumped on my back and sank his choppers in my neck. I managed to elbow Tarzan in the face and swung round and kicked him between his loincloth.

The monkey had already retreated onto the carousel and was giving me the arm from the saddle of pinky pony. By now a crowd of astonished people had gathered and were booing me, (yeah like you did in Woburn safari park when his cousin pulled your fucking aerial off). The monkey then climbed to the top of a pylon and sat there, taking the piss. I did think about jumping into the jet and shooting him down like in King Kong but security were on their way, so I lurched and stumbled away like Joseph Merrick. I gave cuddles the look that inferred I was coming back with a blunderbuss.

After visiting the Red Cross tent, I was whisked off to the local hospital where I spent two hours in A&E having tetanus injections and a debriefing from a vet. The old Bill arrived and asked me if I wanted to press charges against the fair owners, thinking about it, the only thing fair in a fair is the name. I considered it, then declined. It turned out the monkey was a minor anyway. I heard he got off with a reprimand and was sent to his tyre with no tea bags.

At 7 pm, I rejoined the mayhem in the main tent. It took me a while to find the lads, who then dismissed my story as a joke until I showed them my chomp marks. OK, it was chimp, not an orangutan or a gorilla, but people like fucking Clint Eastwood and Attenborough have got plenty to answer for, just ask the population of Hartlepool.

Russian Roulette

After two days of abusing the body and getting up to the usual things on a stag do, like chaining our mate and groom, the Crowman, to a stuffed bear (he was lucky, we were going to chain him to a tram.) We also filled his underpants with wet cement whilst he was heavily snoring one night, but the room was too hot, and it didn't set.

I bet the chambermaid thought, "Fuck me, That's was a rough masala."

Late on Sunday night our group of twenty-odd had mainly drifted apart. Myself and Rick found ourselves in some sort of Pub Club.

Now I'm not sure how this came about, as it wasn't rehearsed, but if you've ever seen the movies Dirty Rotten Scoundrels, Fiddler on the Roof and Carry on Dr Shipman, well Rick borrowed bits from all of them.

We were sitting at a small table with beer in hand, having a quiet moment just observing the other customers. Next to us were a couple, I'd say they looked in their mid-40s. The guy was a Bamber Gascoigne clone in open university uniform of cor- duroy's, arm patches and had a Tefal styled cranium. She was a petite blonde in denim with a bit of a sauerkraut face. She later introduced herself as Dolly, and she certainly made up for her cabbage snout by carrying Parton's treasure chest.

Anyway, we smiled and exchanged nods, and then Bamber leaned forward and asked us something in French. Uh? We didn't answer we just gave a friendly shrug. So in English he tried again.

"Do you come here before gentlemen?" He enquired in Poirot accent.

I didn't know what Rick was thinking, but I just replied in a dodgy Russian accent.

"Niet, we are coming on a ship from St Petersburg; my name is Sergio, and this is Richolas."

Rick pressed his foot on mine under the table.

"Oh, are you in the Navy?" Asked Dolly.

"Da, Navy is good." I said.

Then Rick butted in, "We brothers, we Roosky err. . . Cossacks, you know, dancing men from Kiev?"

He crossed his legs did a little shuffle and lifted his arms.

"Hey," he shouted.

They applauded politely.

"Oh really?" Said Bamber (real name Yanis) with a wry smile, "How interesting."

The small talked continued, and I explained Rick's English was not too good and not to buy him a drink (as he'd just offered) because he has a problem when he drinks too much.

"Oh really?" Said Yanis again.

"Yes," I continued. "When he is drunk he is transported back to a ten-year-old boy."

This gave Rick more ammo. As the night wore on, we continually dug holes for ourselves. I couldn't believe the shit we were coming out with. Add to that, this couple were trivial pursuit champions, and they knew more about Russia and the Soviet Union than Karl Marx.

As we consumed more and more alcohol, I remember thinking this couple are a bit strange. Why are they falling for and lapping up this crap? Is there something more sinister afoot?

Rick returned from the toilet sporting his Rainman look of forward brushed hair and buttoned up polo shirt. He took his seat looking rather mischievous in a slightly insane way and then went full-tilt mode. I have to say this couple could certainly put it away. They ordered a round of shots and Rick downed his immediately and lobbed the class backwards, suddenly switching to Topol. First, he announced to Yanis:

"I like your woman friend, and I want to sexy her! Can doing this OK? Russian man like stallion."

I buried my face in my hands, then interrupted.

"No, no Rick, this is very rude."

Ignoring me, he kept on.

"I vont to climb your beautiful mountains, I love you, Dolly, your tits are like the Kremlin."

He then put a wad of Francs on the table. I grimaced and shut one eye. Fuck me, Rick, you've gone too far this time.

"Rick this is Yanis's wife, not a friend." I said, reproachfully.

The thing was she just laughed.

Then Yanis said, "This is all very amusing gentlemen, and I find your little performance entertaining but perhaps you would be interested to know our occupation?"

"You're not old bill?" Rick asked in a Luton accent.

"Niet, Niet." I said, kicking his leg.

"No Rick, not the police. We are doctors of psychology."

He pulled out a card and gave it to me. Fucking hell Rita, we've been done up like a Flemish kipper. Rick started laughing like the clown on the pier for a couple of minutes then spoke in broad Bedfordshire.

"Here Dolly, do you like drumming?"

"Yes, I love all sorts of music, do you play Rick?" She replied teasingly.

"Da," replied Rick.

In a flash, he jumped up on the stage and became Keith Moon, bashing the resident drum kit. I had to bite on my arm; it certainly was a show stopper. 150 people just froze and stared. I stood up and grabbed his arm.

"No, no, come down Rick."

Then security arrived. I remonstrated but to no avail. "Shit it's gonna go pear-shaped," I thought.

I pleaded with them, "Look he's OK, no problem."

"I'll get his straight jacket, it's in the car."

Lacking humour, the bouncers grabbed Rick and pulled him off the stage. Yanis stood up and in defence of Rick, who was about to be thrown down the stairs, assured the men in black with local patter that Rick was a case study and tagged. Well, probably nothing like that, but whatever he said, it did the trick. We all sat down again. Rick was looking sheepish, he winked at me, gripping Dolly's hand. It was getting out of control; more drinks arrived from Bamber's wallet. This time a bottle of Mumm.

"Right, we are gonna have to come clean," I thought, "The joke's wearing thin and Rick is OTT."

Then the disco started up and to my concern, Dolly led Rick to the dancefloor, she was slaughtered and so was he as they stumbled around the floor with a wedding waltz to London Beat. I looked at the floor shaking my head then up at Yanis who came and sat next me. Hang on, hang on, WTF?

He then put his hand on my knee and whispered "Sergio, or whatever your real name is, do you swing?"

Errrrr... shocked, but knowing what he meant, I deflected his question with "yeah love jazz, cool."

"Listen, my friend," he continued, "My wife wants Rick, and I want you, we have an apartment not far."

I nearly swallowed my tongue as I choked, "Sorry, what did you say?"

He repeated his proposition. . . so after inhaling very deeply, I calmly said, at a 100 miles an hour, "Look mate, I need to own up, we're English on a stag weekend we were just having a laugh with you and your Mrs, I'm sorry for this but it's got ridiculous; we're not interested, sorry."

I shifted back on my chair and looked at him, his face had become a touch fiendish looking if he had a beard he could have been Fagin. Slightly disappointed, he agitatedly replied, "You think I am stupid with your games all night? I know you are English fools and, by the way, If you are going lie, learn your geography, Kiev is in the Ukraine. But it is of no consequence."

He stared at me, like a Bond villain, "I still like you, he said, and if you like my friend, we can swap. My wife likes to be cuckold; maybe that is your preference?"

He touched my hand and said, cavalier style, "Come on my friend, you will enjoy."

Fucking hell, this was getting dangerous. By now he had the look of a Flemish Fred West, plus Belgium is always on the news for mass perverted sex murders and added to that the fact that I never read his card properly, he could be the butcher of Brussels. I made a quick excuse and said I needed to go for a leak and would be back soon. I passed Rick and whispered into his shell-like.

"Code Red, Code Red, let's get the fuck out of here."

I put a big emphasis on the next word, "Now."

But Rick was so pissed all he could do was bury his face in Dolly's tits. In the toilet, I sat on the bog. "This calls for a special forces strategy," I thought.

Mobile phones were still in their infancy and although I had my Vodafone it only worked for SOS calls not SAS calls. So turning into a man of action, I steamed out of the toilet, made a beeline for Rick and bundled him across the floor and into a table, knocking people everywhere. We then tripped down the stairs. The bouncers thought a fight had broken out, and indeed it had. My actions sparked a mini wild west saloon Belgian bust up. I just grabbed Rick and shook him as we lay sprawled on the bottom of the stairs.

"Listen, we are in serious shit," I said, "We have got to get out of here, no time to explain."

"Really?" He said, disorientated.

"110%" I replied with a face straighter than Watling Street.

We pushed our way through to the bar door and legged it up the road with some of the security in tow. After running through several alleys, Rick turned and said "Fuck this, I'm tired of running, let's have it."

He quickly reconsidered his statement when he saw four doormen built like Bluto bearing down on us. We ran again through a maze of alleys, then, knackered, I pulled Rick left into a doorway, and we crashed through into a sex shop. It was empty except for the spaced out mascara overload of a stoner manager who had obviously been checking out his new stock! He zipped his flies and looked up.

I just put my finger to my lips, slung 30 Francs on the counter and whispered "Fucking cops man."

We hid behind the latest gas masks then after ten minutes of trying to get our breath back we staggered over and leaned on his counter. I explained the full SP to Rick and Alice Cooper adding that the old Bill were in pursuit.

"Jesus," said Rick.

"You're joking man," said the stoner, "Fuck the pigs!"

"He nearly did." I said, pointing to Rick.

We thanked the manager for his understanding and the joint.

"No problem guys."

As he launched into a monologue regarding his dislike for uniformed pork, we left stealthily, dodging through more alleys. Police sirens were wailing in the distance, were they connected to us? I doubt it. We ambled along for a bit then slid into an old fishermen's bar, ordered a sea shanty then collapsed laughing.

Rick said, "I wished we could have filmed it all, this's been a fucking blinding night."

In hindsight maybe I should have taken Dolly back."

"Oh yeah," I said sarcastically, "We could've ended up being in Hannibal Lector's freezer, wearing a gimp mask."

"You mean you could've."

The next morning we relayed our story to the others at breakfast as we discussed the meaning of my wife likes a cuckold.

"Must be some sort of Belgium chocolate." Said Dave, authoritatively.

Just to be on the safe side, and obviously not to draw attention to ourselves, we visited a joke shop and boarded the ferry home disguised as 14th-century priests.

CHAPTER 6

Up, Up and Away

Whoever said "Air travel could be the last fortress of solitude" never flew with me.

It used to be for me, and probably you, that airline travel was glamorous, exciting and after delivering Milk Tray, the second most thrilling thing known to mankind. Unfortunately for me nowadays it's become rather laborious and tedious.

Although online check-in has made the initial stage of flying a bit easier, going through security has become a pain. Of course, I realise in today's climate it is a necessity semi-evil, with the sales of Pandora's box outstripping Samsonite, but it still agitates me.

Once on board, and after elbowing several people in the

face, I settle down for blast off. I try not to clock watch, and because I never manage to sleep, even if I'm in business class, I try to break my flight time by dividing it into a Skybox package, of flicks, feeding, fidgeting then flushing.

I've almost lost count of the years I've wasted with my head sat in the clouds or sat on Thomas Crapper. Indeed, I must have flown to the Moon and back several times, and I can tell you there is no cheese! Only dust, a dead cow and a rusting iron chicken.

Add to that the mile high club has never opened its doors to me and I wish I had chosen to collect air miles back in the day, and not Green Shield Stamps, which of course nowadays are worth less than a Jim'll fix it chair.

In retrospect, I reckon with well over 400 flights completed, I could have earned enough points to go on the piss with a Klingon.

Today the majority of air travel and indeed the sky, has been taken over by low-cost carriers. Sleazyjet, one of the first, I worked for when they first limped into the sky with two 737/200's Charlie Hotel/Golf. In fact, I'm still looking for aspirin for my hangover from the early Stellios parties.

Their concept to begin with was great, and by modelling themselves on South West in the States they brought cheap and accessible air travel to the UK masses. But as the Jam sang "what a catalyst you turned out to be," as there are now fewer clouds in the sky than budget airlines and the birds are stuck in Berkeley square.

With all the add-on's nowadays I reckon you may as well pay the extra and fly with a national carrier. I was reading the other day, they were actually considering charging for a no.2! That's a turd, not an air hostess. Would that be by weight? "So let's see sir, your fare is an extra £60 I'm afraid as its a triple S class," which breaks-down for a seat, a suitcase and sewerage. Hey, I have a better idea, why not charge for a window seat with a view or discount people with BYO seat belts, no hang on even better! Let's run an ad campaign. Guaranteed funeral expenses and a free pen for satnav error, stray missiles, bombs or locked cockpit doors!

Nowadays in pond life (economy) it's all about the bass (sorry wrong fish) sardine cabin configurations, which generally means you need to assume the brace position just to open your boiled sweet. Don't they realise people have arms and legs? Another thing, some of them dump you at such a remote airport it's quicker sitting by the exit (salida) door with a parachute. (I always wondered for years why they sold salad by a toilet). But Look having said all that, I do realise and can relate to the attraction for punters of this very successful business model. So despite my indifference I will be shortly launching a rival to Easyjet in the same livery with Simon's Space Hoppers!

The following pages contain recollections of some of my more eventful flights. Rather similar to always having a set of stairs handy to replace the ambulance lift when the scheduled flight to Lourdes from Luton Airport used to return, I think that, however jaded over the decline in the fun of commercial air travel I become, l will never totally loose faith in miracles.

Muppets

In late '93 I decided to fly from LHR to Sydney via Amsterdam, this came about during a gardening retail therapy trip to London when I entered a bucket shop but ended up with an air ticket.

Fast forward to Amsterdam where I'm flicking through the porn at Schiphol newsstands waiting for KLM 507.

At 0930 I quickly knocked one out in the toiletten, then boarded the Pride of Rotterdam around 10ish, a bit early for a J Arthur I know, but shame to waste my new razzle.

The plane was full as it was travelling onto NZ. I was seated in the middle of two muppets, God I hate being trapped. To my right was Kermit and to my left Ms. Piggy,

I changed very brief pleasantries with my fellow puppets and was informed by Piggy that her name was Lucy. She was a child of the sixties, a hippie chick if you like. Kermit the frog, was more a Parisian toad actually, he introduced himself as Bruno.

After the initial climb Piggy had started to weep and slobber, water streamed down her face like she was troughing the biggest bags of onions. She was pitifully gazing at a picture of some eastern guru, a bit like a '90s version of Russell Brand. Other passengers started to look at me like I had told her she looked fat in cheesecloth! Then the stewardess was on the case.

After a brief chat, it transpired she was a disillusioned Australian who had been traded in Goa by Andy Gandhi for a new model, and half a bag of skunk weed. She now faced being resigned to returning home to put nappies on orphaned Joeys in Wagga Wagga.

To cheer her up, the hostie brought her grub early, she tucked into Linda McCartney's reheated sausages and at 36,000 feet the smell was rank. It suddenly dawned on me, 'So that's what happens to Sir Paul's old underpants'. Ahh! Not a Bisto kid in sight. She looked at me for Ideas. I shrugged, but in Commonwealth camaraderie I offered her a Rolo. She ungratefully folded her arms looking pissed off and snapped "Cosmic."

Meanwhile to my right sat the upright amphibian, he was wearing a black beret embellished with the Israeli army badge and had turned up his collars on his beige rain mac. He was browsing a French magazine called Ski Telemark. It had pictures of a man in a dinner suit holding a revolver like James Bond on Mont Blanc. So putting two and two together, I came up with twenty-two, and that he was a not so undercover secret service operative. Failing that, he was a fan of Some Hebrew Mothers do Ave Em. My racing mind returned to my seat as our meals arrived.

"Le rôti de boeuf?" The hostess asked Kermit.

"Non, Poisson."

He wasn't far wrong there, my experience of airline food is that unless you're in business, it's on par with lunch at my old junior school.

Suddenly my litter tray was plonked in front of me, Piggy turned and gave me a look of disdain and muttered something. I surveyed my lunch, then glanced at Bruno, who was foreskin-ing his fish, then Piggy leant forward and turned to me again this time with pursing snotter and re-grunted. I adjusted my volume down to number 3. Time for some sarcasm!

"Sorry, did you say something? I didn't catch that I was listening to the Smiths, I recommend them." I said rather loudly as you do when wearing headphones.

"Murderaar," she replied in that Aussie drawl.

I revolved my head like the girl in the Exorcist to check if she was aiming it at somebody else. Nope, it was definitely me.

Again she snorted "Murderaar! Meat is murder." She repeated.

'Oh, that old chestnut from Wings', I thought. "So you are listening to Morrissey?" I continued "Oh well, maybe you should retune to channel five. Francis Bacon's frying his latest theory."

My meal arrived. I peeled back the foil on my Sunday dinner. Slices of Angus lay lifeless on a bed of noodles; my tray also had a variety of small boxes that had even less appeal. I met her gaze and licked my lips, then turned up my volume again. 'Oh now it's her favourite band' I thought, 'Ugly Kid Joe!'

I picked up my starter, then juggled a sliver of salmon onto my spoon. She suddenly grabbed my wrist with her trotter, then pulled at my earpiece, a statement quickly followed.

"If you could see what goes on in a slaughterhouse mate, you'd never eat meat again, you fucking sadist."

What? With more self-control than a Nun trying not to shoplift candles as her batteries had run out, I removed her cloven hoof.

Why is she picking on me? There are 400 other passengers tucking into Aberdeen's finest. Just because that little piggy wasn't having roast beef. The Ashes were back on, Beefy Botham v Skippy the Kangagorillapig.

I picked up my piece of citrus and rung its neck but as I squeezed life out of her my lemon. It sent a tiny jet of juice with the precision and trajectory of a guided laser straight into the left eye of the Bruno.

"Sacre bleu," he shrieked, keeping to the script.

"Man down, man down," I radioed in. Then sprang into action, but unfortunately I knocked his coffee over his crotch.

"INCOMING" I warned. Too late. He shot up like Tom the cat and banged his beret on the overhead.

"Sorry mate," I gestured.

"Ooh la la Betty," he retorted.

In the commotion, a voice came from my left "Desole or je suis desole?" It was the concerned stewardess, who was already on the case. I presumed this meant are you OK. With all this pandemonium the 747 suddenly did a loop the loop, when all the passengers stood up behind me to see what was going on.

OK I made that bit up, but you could've lit a fat cigar off my cheeks or given me an exploding one, as you could still smoke in those days.

I grovelled apologetically, like the melon eating Indian Michael Cane threw off the train at Marwar Junction in The Man who would be King. If you haven't seen the movie, let's just say I was more sorry than the man who gave Nick Leeson a job.

The stewardess did her best to wipe Bruno/Kermit down and brought a portable hair dryer, she then proceeded to blast his crotch. A new meaning for Wind in the Willows came to mind. After an eye bath and a change of Lili Pad, Bruno recovered.

Piggy had now changed from Napoleon in Animal Farm to Mother Theresa in Oh Calcutta. She turned her pedals, and started up her erroneous cycle then added chanting and mantras all aimed at Bruno.

Somehow I had become invisible; they struck up a brief speed dating conversation, which basically went. Hi, my name's Lucy, where are you going? What do you do? That's very interesting. Can I shag you?

"Non, Je Suis navre, I bat for the other side!"

Normal service was resumed. Piggy, disappointed again at being rejected, floated off into a crestfallen trance then met up with Buddha on the wing. Bruno hurriedly settled down to watch his adversary in an old 007 movie, in his case, For half Yours Eyes Only on the neck breaking TV, no seatback screens in those days.

After Piggy awoke she stood up and walked to the rear of the aircraft returning with a small boy of about 12 and the hostess. They had decided to swap her with a U.M. (unaccompanied minor); suits me sir, I thought, as she snatched her kaftan and packet of smokey lentil from my obliging hand.

The kid sat like a crash test dummy for 10 hours without even breathing; he was so scared, poor old boy. This time the stewardess was not on the case. I tried to talk to him, but my Hollandaise was nonexistent. So I changed tact with a set of national stereotype questions. Do you wear clogs? Is Dutch Rarebit, Edam on toast? Then getting fed up with his unwillingness to engage in my best efforts, I said, "Do you know Father Abraham has a blue dick son?"

"I'm from Luxembourg," he said "and how do you know?"

Time for bed said, Zebedee.

Panto-Loons

Summer '94 I'm aboard an old Tri-Star as we bump down at Karachi for refueling.

I'm on my way to Sri Lanka and then Hong Kong to meet the Cat, a good mate who features in later chapters. After what seemed like reading for six hours from June's edition of Tea growing for Tamils, two new passengers presented themselves to the economy.

In front a giant bearded man, who announces in a booming voice.

"Hello, my friends I am the great Baboo."

This giant of a self styled holyman was a ringer for Brian Blessed, with a Turban and jeweled cane. He was followed by his most humble assistant (his words); A praying mantis. Now this man was the tallest, thinnest man I'd ever seen. He reminded me of the alien in Close Encounters; Rumour had it he was from the Twiglet zone.

Baboo looked for a reaction, but people just thought 'Nutter' and carried on reading. Then, I knew it, I just bloody knew it, yes, he came and sat next to me. He had the fucking pick of a least 20 seats and he goes and chooses me. Drat and Double Drat, Muuuutley get me out of here! Fuck it, out of medals again.

Twiglet then sits himself down in the adjacent seat in next aisle.

The steward briskly walked past and requests Baboo to fasten his seat belt but stops and returns to put his stick up and put it in the overhead. Baboo looks at me with his genie smile. The first of my three wishes was going to be: Can you fuck off mate!

Is this for real? I expected another passenger, not a fucking pantomime. Baboo yawned and spread his huge frame and flopped back into recline mode. His seat groaned under the weight.

"Please sir, keep your seat upright until after take-off and the seat belt sign has been extinguished," said another passing steward on automatic.

Baboo turned to me again "Excuse me sir, are you aware of who I am?"

"Er yep you're the GGGreat Baboo." I replied sarcastically.

"That's right my friend", he replies like he's amazed. "Yes the Great Baboo" he continues "Son of Socar. I am a magician, preacher and mountain guide, at your service sir."

"Get many gigs at K2?" I enquired.

Nodding sideways again with a huge smile, he says "Vely good, vely funny ha ha ha. Where are you coming from sir?"

Right, time to be patronising. "I'm From London Baboo; that's England, near Europe, just turn left on the A62 at Turkey, you can't miss it. Cold country with giant castles and fish and chips!"

Oh, lovely, lovely, I love England. I have many friends there."

"Thought you might."

"Do you know my friend, Houdini?" Asked Baboo.

"Er no, not personally," then pausing, "But wasn't he American?"

"You don't know Houdini! Vel bloody blimey."

"Of course, I know who he was!"

"Listen my friend, Houdini was a very big, big, friend of mine. Yes, we go way back in the mists of time." Recalls Baboo, staring into the imaginary mists.

"Oh yeah, well that makes you about 120 then!"

We taxi out and make full use of the runway to lift the ageing old girl up into the air. Ding ding. Baboo repeatedly presses the call button. Eventually, he gets a 'yes sir' from the steward.

"What time is lunch?" Enquires Baboo.

"In about an hour sir." Comes the reply.

Baboo gives the steward a lengthy explanation about being as hungry as a pachyderm and an hour being far too long to wait while teetering on the brink of starvation, while giving a look that says I am really hungry (well as hungry as a 18 stone man can look.) The steward politely listens and then gives Baboo that look that says fuck off you self-important twat.

Within a flash Baboo is snoring. I close my eyes and thank the Lord for his divine intervention. I stood up on my seat and leap over the Khyber pass into the aisle and found solitude six rows back.

Dinner's served, and I pick at my curry and feeding time at the zoo begins. They only had one film, so they repeat Romancing the Stone which even then was at least ten years old. The projector flickers into life.

I reflect the similarity between the movies Romancing and Raiders, and that Baboo should give Spielberg a ring for the sequel. While gazing out the window over mountains, I suddenly see to my horror the reflection of the said Baboo plonking himself next to me again.

"There you are my friend."

I really was starting to get totally pissed off with this guy and getting a bit irate, surely he has missed the 'n' off the end of his name. "Look Baboo your holiness, you seem a nice chap and I'm sure you're playing to packed audiences at the Wheel Tappers and Sherpas, but I want be left alone OK!"

He suddenly turned into Snorbits and rested his St Bernard size head on my shoulder, and gives me the sad eyed dog routine.

"Listen, my friend, I have a vely funny joke for you."

"Go on then." I submit.

After the punchline of the hilarious piece of satire from the sub continent has been delivered, I remark "That's up there with Dave Allen."

Then Salvation. Redemption for all my crimes, suddenly there's an a bing bong and the captain announces:

"Ladies and gentlemen, and not forgetting the Great Baboo, this is Captain Scarlet speaking. We will be shortly making our descent into Bombay. We hope you've had an enjoyable flight, sorry about that cunt in the carpet slippers, but you should have flown with a proper Airline. (Well that's what he should have said)"

"This is my stop, that's my destination." Announces Baboo, at his usual level 11 volume.

A smile as wide as zippy appears on my face. Touchdown. Whoosh, the Circus leaves town. I deflate, exhausted.

Half the aircraft disembarked, a few dozen Chinese haul their 1000 kilo hand luggage up the isle; then we are on our way again to Colombo. At last! After Sri Lanka, the route will then take the plane to Bangkok and then Hong Kong. The same route I will be taking the following week.

I am elated to be only two hours away from Sri Lanka, and despite being alone, I am looking forward to exploring the country with its alleged breathtaking scenery, lovely beaches, exotic food and especially it's civil war.

We level out above the clouds. I open my free newspaper, the Karachi times, English version. Oh, I see Imran made a century, but only against Bangladesh, does that count? I conjecture. Well it's a sort of local derby so I'll allow it.

"Hello, there." A voice sounds behind the paper, "Don't you recognise me?"

Oh for fuck's sake, not again.

"Well, it would help if I could see you!"

A head slowly peers over the sports section.

"No, sorry."

"Don't you work at Lucas Aerospace in Luton, it's Simon right?" Continues the man.

Hang on a tick, I reconsider. Yeah, shit it's er, it's...

"Well blow me, Dr Mucagee" well not literally!

Air fix

Talking of Doctors "If there is a doctor onboard, will he please make himself known to a cabin crew member."

I've heard that one on several occasions over the intercom. Like the time I was flying from Melbourne to Dubai when Istanbul's answer to Mr Creosote had one too many Turkish delights and broke his seat back, crushing my legs, whilst having a heart attack. Or how about the time an intoxicated woman, went berserk mid-Atlantic during heavy turbulence. She tried to open the emergency exit door and had to be given acepromazine, a horse tranquillizer, by Doctor Jekyll to keep her from becoming Mrs. Hyde. Then there was the time a well-endowed flasher on an Air Egypt flight, burst out of the toilet, with his peculiar version of Snakes on a Plane, and that's a dry airline. God knows what he was on. Luckily they served a very nice Bromide mint tea.

But I never thought it would happen to me. OK, I was once taken sick coming back from Agra, India when I felt faint after doing 2 bottles of Cab Sauv but that was self-inflicted.

On this occasion, I had boarded an early Air Asia flight from Bangkok to Kuala Lumpur, when shortly after take-off I went on tilt. As I slid onto the couple next to me and parked myself on a young girl's lap, she panicked and screamed thinking I was wrecked, but I was heaving serious heart arrhythmia. The air hostess was hopeless, as many of the low-cost carrier hosties are, they are just kids and chosen in Asia mainly on their looks, not their abilities. I am not saying they have failed their line checks, or that their cabin manager has not stringently passed them off, but when a real emergency happens, and with little experience, sometimes their professionalism is left wanting.

After being treated by a handy US army paramedic, the plane diverted and touched down at Hat Yai, a southern city in Thailand.

The ambulance was waiting as I was manhandled down the stairs and onto a makeshift ironing board, only to be lobbed into the back of a Toyota pickup/ hot dog van.

So with sirens and lights a blazing, we set off with the deafening accompaniment of the soothing vibes of NWA hip-hop. Lying on my stretcher I remember thinking this resembles the inside of a club more than an ambulance.

A bearded female nurse was holding my pulse with one hand whilst doing her eyeshadow with the other. Her companion; the chain-smoking Dr Dre, took the wheel. "Dum, dum, fuck the police," repeated the speakers. "Bump, bump, fuck the patient," I repeated.

We arrived at the private hospital, The Bangkok Hat Yai, a very plush and extremely expensive hospital chain in Thailand, who's ethos is more aimed towards a luxury hotel rather than clinical.

I was transferred to my all singing, all dancing bed, which was previously owned by Inspector Gadget. The door opened and in walked the consultant, Dr Sirrapoon, aka Dr Doolittle, a very apt name, he mumbled something, scratched his arse and walked off.

The nurse then took some ECG's, some small notes, some medium blood, some large x-rays, and a huge sum of large notes: Money.

It's 7 pm; I'm standing outside the hospital with mobile in hand explaining to the Mrs and then my dad that I could have stayed the night, but they didn't except worry beads.

I wandered the streets looking for a mid-class hotel. The City of HatYai borders the three southern provinces of Thailand. These areas are adjoined to Malaysia and are involved in a religious independence dispute. Like so many of these places at present they're not advisable to visit. However mine was unplanned.

The street was full of army personnel, which kind of reassured me as I checked into Orchid Lodge. It had a hideous, garish foyer with statues of dragons and mythical creatures, all wrapped in red Chinese bamboo patterned wallpaper. Four clocks adorned the reception wall with Bangkok, London, Beijing and Lima highlighted, a strange combination I remarked to myself, perhaps Paddington bear was in the penthouse.

The price was only £15 a night, with breakfast and extra marmalade. Oh, bollocks that will do, I thought, it's now 9 pm. Oh, and I must remember to get a taxi booked for 5 am to get me to Alo Star Airport, which is just inside the Malaysian border to continue my journey.

THE SEARCH FOR THE GOOSE'S PALM

The Air Asia rep had told me they would give me a free ride onto KL, as long as I was on the 07:30 flight.

The Room was basic but appeared clean, the bathroom had a few dead bodies but none of them human. The Satellite TV picture was very snowy and needed a good wash with Head and Shoulders, but I could hear BBC 24 news, but still no mention of me.

I decided, against my better judgement, that I would explore the hotel for an hour, so I had a quick splash in the Shower and off I went. On the way down I was stopped six times by various staff offering massage, I just smiled and marched myself head down into the bar and karaoke lounge.

This was to be another surreal experience, with a collection of the weirdest creatures that had never appeared on Dr Who. Countless ladyboys and trannies, ranging from 'yeah I'd give that one if I were pissed', to 'didn't I see you in Mrs. Doubtfire' lounged around the seating area. The other male population, i.e., the guests, were mainly from east of the Rhine. There was a Eurasian Christopher Lee lookalike with a Labrador, aka, (the man with the golden retriever). Two German twins stood at the bar with shiny suits and faces to match the foyer, clones of Siegfried and Roy (post mauled). There was also a pipe smoking Mandarin dwarf wearing a tangerine jumper, probably named Jaffa.

Dr Mengele glared across the bar at me. I glared back with my best fuck off you Nazi stare. The place had a toxic aroma of cheap perfume, sweet tobacco, and feline piss coming from the plague of underfed feral cats, who purred around the shoes of

Imelda Marcos, the entertainments officer. The barman's name was Khun (Mr) Sakdar, aka Jimmy, who was, I have to say, was the only sane one in the place. I ordered a Tiger; that's a beer (the German brothers ran for it) and a tiger's penis, that's a club sandwich. Then I pulled up a stool.

My limp sandwich arrived, typical, all salad no penis. I sat back to enjoy the sweet harmonies of Imelda with Thai a lellow libbon, when a gaggle of transsexuals approached me.

"Sorry ladies, I'm gay," I said immediately (a sort of a contradiction in its self), no problem.

With a click of their nuts, they were replaced by about a dozen pink underpants clad young men. They appeared grinning like a synchronized swimming team and proceeded to climb on the stage and shoot firecrackers from their arses in my direction, never fails to impress that one!

I'm not sure my heart can take this, I thought. Two of them jumped down and snuggled up to me.

"Wooah, just hold your horses thar boys" I said, John Wayne style. I continued with, "Thank you for all your attention, but I am a priest."

Fuck knows where that came from, it even made me laugh, but it also made no difference as they slid their oily hands all over me.

"Jimmy, help me out here," I called over to the bar, holding my hands up like a stick-up. Jimmy said something that I didn't understand, even though my Thai is passable, but it did the trick, and they sloped off back to other guests.

"Kop Khun Marg" (thanks very much) Jimmy," I said.

"No problem Mr Simon. We chatted from English to Thai, then he said, "You really priest?"

I explained the situation that I was on my way to KL for a visa run. In those days my yearly visa meant I had to leave Thailand every three months to get it stamped, he seemed to understand.

"Listen, Khun Simon," he whispered, "I have nice lady! Can come up your loom, vely lovely and sexy and vely cheap!"

"Er, no thanks mate."

I told him I was married plus I had to get up very early the next day but thanked him all the same. He wouldn't let it go.

"No problem khun Simon, tell her go four clock, she my sister, vely good boom boom, and only 19."

"Look Jimmy," I tried again. "Thanks and all, but I just came in here for a beer and a snack, but seem to have ended up with the cast from the Rocky Horror Picture show!"

"Mai Khao jai" he said (I don't understand)

"Don't matter mate, here's 200 Baht for the company (£5)."

I returned to my room, dodging the extra guests wandering around the corridors; maybe they should have called it Hotel California after the Eagles tune, but hopefully I could leave!

I was awoken by the sound of two stroke engines farting outside, shit, its 6.15 how did that happen? I ordered a wake call for 5am. Puzzled, I checked the phone, fuck it, dead. With the Speed of Gonzales I was outside, juggling my half open bag in under a minute, and clambering into a beat-up Proton Taxi conveniently parked by a soup stall.

"Sa-wat-dee Khrap, (Alright mate), Alo Star Airport Malaysia, as fast as you can please," I said in Thai.

Although I added "big tip, big tip," the taxi guy said even at Mach 11, it was still about 2 hours away plus a 30 min wait at the border. I made a joke about Chitty, Chitty Bang Bang, which fell on deaf ears. (No toot sweets for him), so I just slumped back and tried to call Air Asia on my mobile. The reception was hopeless and kept breaking up, after three unsuccessful attempts to explain to the twat at the other end, I went all Eurovision, and just said "Good evening, Bangkok, this is Copenhagen calling, we award Thailand nil point, and Cambodia douze (12) points."

After a major hold up at the border, where the car was searched three times and my paperwork was examined with a Thai tooth-comb, I was fined 1500 Baht for some imaginary offence, even though I had a letter from the hospital plus Air Asia stating that I had a medical emergency. Sympathy, like fresh water, is in short supply in Thailand, it's all about the dollar, or Baht should I say.

The driver was also fined 500B for smoking contraband that paid for the Border Police's breakfast, which I might add the driver added onto my fare as an excise tax. Once we crossed into Malaysia normal service was resumed, but by the time we got to the Airport, it was gone 9 am.

After remonstrating with the Air Asia rep, and even though I knew from my Easyjet days it would be fruitless arguing, I managed to get a small refund, and rebooked myself on Malaysian airlines flight MS278 to KL departing 1120.

I must admit I felt a little nervous boarding after all the problems of my last flight, but I was pleasantly surprised. The plane was almost empty, and the flight crew were excellent and attentive, the hostesses dressed in their emerald uniform's looked good enough for lunch, so I invited them. I arrived at KL and transferred to the 5 star Shangri-la Hotel, downtown and spent a most enjoyable four nights in the company of the green goddesses.

CHAPTER 7

Forz's Wedding and a Funnel

Fuck, fuck, fuck it, fuckity fuck, bugger, bollocks.

No, I'm not late for a wedding, but I've just spilled my breakfast coffee over my boiled eggs, and I'm not wearing any underpants. Thinking about it though, I reckon I could give Hugh Grant a run for his money.

OK, maybe not in two hours, but I've got a few gigs under my belt. From the humble jug bar of the local working mans' club to the grandeur of Sydney Opera House and many more.

If you peruse my wedding C.V, you'll notice I have offered my services in many capacities. These include the groom's side kick (thrice), a planner, an usher, a chauffeur, and I've even been known to cater a reception or two.

So whether it be civic or churchly, white or shotgun, straight or gay, I would like to think there's enough material in my head for the largest of brides. When I was younger I did a bit of scuba diving; now there's an interesting concept, underwater unification.

"Ladies and gentleman, please be up-floating for Mr and Mrs Nemo."

Talking of unusual weddings, I did once attend a Chinese ghost marriage, where two deceased people dressed in cardboard suits spirit bonded. The description extremely bizarre is not adequate, and I have to say I didn't think much of the best man's speech.

With having so many unions to select from I was going to knock up a wheel of fortune and leave the needle to pick you out a story that meets the criteria for this book. In other words, one that happened while travelling. However, after long deliberation I have chosen Ladyboy Godiva on a wild card entry, as it was an Indian wedding, and National Express chipped in.

Unfortunately, this means I don't have enough ink for the other tales, such as Viva Lost Vegas. A fine story about blackjack, an aptly named Afro-American guy from Atlanta who I met in a downtown Vegas bar. He had lost all his money, so he borrowed ten bucks from me so he could get hitched, (a likely story).

There is also Jamaica Inn, no, not Daphne de Maurier, but a Sandals Beach extravaganza set in the 5 star Hotel at Ocho Rios. In this instance, the groom teamed up with Captain

Morgan and I the night before and left his mark on the ceremony when he sprayed the outlaws with projectile vomit.

Last and least, there's my Tie wearing, tying the knot, Thai wedding. Regrettably, all these fables will now have to be saved for the Richard Curtis sequel in the vaults of my flash drive.

If you're wondering about the funnel in the heading, it refers to my big fat Greek funeral. When in Kos, my friend and I mistakenly attended a burial at sea instead of the disco boat.

More of that later, but first I'm sending you to Coventry.

It was a Saturday in mid-July 1995, and the whole UK basked in Wedgwood skies. Ranjit Mahazafore, a work colleague, affectionately known to the boys as Forz was getting hitched. The city of Coventry, incidentally, strangely twinned with Stalingrad had been swapped in a cultural exchange with Amritsar, as Anand Karaj was coming to town.

Anand Karaj means blissful union or in English, Sikh wedding, but this day was not only to be a day of matrimonial celebration for Forz and his bride, but it would also double as an introduction to a new bit of fanny. Yep, Sabel the Tranny was showing out.

To cut a long story short, back in the days of mad cow's disease, aka Girl Power, I was employed in the aerospace industry. I worked in the section involved with the production of aircraft windows with a small team of around fourteen, mainly guys with a couple of females, Oh, and Sharky.

The lads and I always new Sharky had some dark hidden secret. He was a chameleon of a character at work and rather

THE SEARCH FOR THE GOOSE'S PALM

introvert. You wouldn't even notice he was there sometimes, as he would quietly blend into the background. However, come four thirty he would transform by the lockers to an extrovert, donning a Marilyn Manson t-shirt and plenty of mascara with attitude.

He may have been gay, so what! So why did he go out of his way in conversations to slate off Jimmy Somerville or any other bummers, as he called them, playing on the radio? Perhaps it was to camouflage his uncomfortable feeling towards his sexuality, as he often displayed some effeminate traits.

When questioned about his use of Boots number 7, or Manson's preference for arse, he would defend it with, "Look, it's a fashion statement. Plus it really pisses my dad off, who's a German cunt!"

Then one Friday morning at a start-up meeting, in waltzed Sharky with HR and the Foreman and made an audacious announcement.

"Achtung Baby, today we say goodbye to Sharky, as I step out of my double closet, and as of this moment my new name will be Sable Stark. I am, for my sins, a born again transsexual. Oh, if anyone's interested I will be auctioning off my fruit and veg and from Monday I'll be in high heels."

Well, most of the chaps were surprised, but not totally shocked. Unfortunately, Christina, a fifty-something devout Irish Catholic, decided he was the antichrist and hailed Mary, then a cab and promptly left the company. Oh, and the foreman asked for his safety shoes back.

Ranjit's wedding date had caused a bit of a dilemma, as it

clashed with the annual works freebie summer do, which was always a good hoot. So Chris, a work college and good friend, and I, decided in our wisdom to do both. By firstly attending the wedding by day and then returning to Luton about sixish for the company knees-up.

We thought our plan was a good compromise, as Indian weddings sometimes go on for days. Plus it was a chance for Sharky/Sable to show off his new VPL to the girls and gets tips on phantom PMT from Kim in wages.

The big day had arrived. Chris and I waited in apprehension on my sofa for the arrival of Sable, who I will refer to from now on as he/him, Because we found out later he was still pre-op at the time. Although we had pretty readily accepted Sable's new identity, we still were a little uneasy at taking him to his first ball as Cindafella.

Ding dong, said the front door. I gave Chris the nod then braced myself as I opened up to a vision of beastly. Bloody hell it's boy Georgina!

With raised eyebrows, but definitely nothing else, I led him into the front room where an uncomfortable thirty seconds silence ended when Chris just burst into hysterics. Sable's face blended into his red carnation; Chris spluttered an apology, and then we all cracked up again.

The problem for Chris and I was that Sable had an awful 6 o'clock shadow and despite having electrolysis and being caked in foundation, he just looked like a drag queen. In fact, I heard a rumour last year that he went on to win Eurovision for Austria.

We set off for Coventry by WV Polo, with Sable behind the wheel and me as co-driver. Chris sat on the back seat and said nothing, his face contorted with the effort of trying to hold his sniggers.

Sable clunked the gears. "Sorry," he said, "Not used to driving with 6-inch heels!"

Chris started again. For me, it was no big deal as I'd seen a plenty of ladyboys in Thailand, so I didn't give a fuck. Although, I have to admit as I already hinted I would have had to be completely shitfaced to fancy Sable. We arrived at a big mother of a Sikh temple, The Sri Guru.

The wedding was a huge affair with about 300 guests including local dignitaries and VIP's. With so many colourful sarees, Sable blended in perfectly in her multicoloured Topshop outfit and was getting plenty of attention from the girls, camcorders and the snake charmer.

The Bride arrived by horse and carriage, and after a few processions of elephants, parasols, and banging drums, she entered the Temple. Chris suggested to Sable that he should strip off and ride the horse around town like Lady Godiva did eons ago.

"Just thought as zee TV is here, and we're in Coventry mate, it would be a great advertisement for gender reassignment," said Chris.

"I think you'll find it was a white horse bitch, not my little pony." Sable replied. "Hark at her. How about lady muff diver then?" I joked.

"Thanks, but no thanks, that's for your tongue Simon." Rebuffed Sable.

He continued. "From now on it's got to be meaty, beauty, big and bouncy!"

It was a brief ceremony, which surprised me. Then a trumpet sounded. "Grub's up." Said someone. We entered, and sat down on the floor for our feast with some of our other work colleges that had travelled up by mini bus, around eighteen in total.

We were assigned table number nine; borrowed from some cricket club with a short leg. The older males of our party started whining. First it was, "The food's nothing like as good as The Royal Tandoori in Dunstable." Followed by, "Why do we have to sit on the floor?"

"Don't they have chairs in Delhi?" Said Bob, "I've already crossed my legs for two hours holding a piss in on the coach." It went on. "The Glasses are dirty; the wine's not very cold." And the final and biggest complaint was the fact we had to eat with our hands.

"Oi, this is a Sikh wedding, not dinner at the palace." Barked dog's breath, real name Gerry Smith. He continued. "You lot should enter into the spirit of the occasion, you old fossils."

"Hear, hear," I added in my best Westminster voice.

Mind you the soup was difficult! Later, after the English had finished their tea party, the mess was cleared away.

"Bloody Jatts (peasants)," I heard one of the waiters say.

His co-worker agreed to mutter about 'low class people'. "Low seats." I thought.

By now my back was starting to cramp up, so I decided it was time to stand up before I welded myself into the lotus position.

The music then changed from background sitar twanging to; *Now That's what I call Punjabi, volume 2.* The rest of my work colleagues were press-ganged into dancing. They looked very uncomfortable and reminiscent of unenthusiastic '70s audiences on *Top of the Pops*.

There was a line forming for what I thought was going to be the Coventry conga, but I soon realised it was the cue to wash your hands. Suddenly the ante was upped, as smoke and flashing lights began. DJ Bombay mix woke up the ancestors and frightened the elderly with hardcore Bangla; then everybody was up doing the *Oi, Oi, my heads on fire* dance.

After 20 minutes, I was knackered. I smouldered back to the bar. By now Sable had become the centre of attention again and was trying on headscarves and bangles, this gave Chris and me some respite as minders, so we went outside for a joint.

"What's the time mate?" I enquired.

"Err 5:32." Chris replied.

"Bloody hell! I said. "We'd better rescue Jemima Khan and get moving, or we'll miss tonight."

We hurriedly looked out Forz and his new bride and thanked them for their hospitality. I wanted to stay really, as by now the girls had changed into western clothes, and there were some very fit Bollywood babes. Disappointed, I dragged Sable away and bid farewell to the grumpy English, still sat huddled in a circle like the condemned in a re-enactment of the White Hole of Calcutta.

Sable needed five minutes to retape his shrivelled knackers, so Chris quickly changed from his formals into a LA Raiders t-shirt and jeans. I decided to stay in my Alexei Sayle suit (That's the comedian, not a discounted two piece). Sable fired up the Polo and off we set. I started up a run of the mill conversation.

"So you haven't hadn't had the chop then yet, mate?'

"No," Sable replied, "I have to wait for my last meeting with the nut doctor. Going to Barnet next Tuesday."

"What, do they have a special doctor in Cockfosters?" Laughed Chris.

"No, I mean a psychiatrist, they have to check I'm not insane/nuts before they start slicing." Said Sable.

"So what's all this shit about your Dad then?" Chris asked.

"Well, he always hated me, since I was a baby. Then In my puberty, he caught me several times in mum's clothes. and being a fucking Nazi beat the shit out of me."

"Should have dressed in an SS uniform." I joked.

Just then, about ten minutes into the M45, the car started to kangaroo.

"What's up Doc?" I said to Sable.

"Dunno" he replied.

"It's not fuel; there's half a tank." Said Chris.

Then there was a loud bang, and the car died. Not being a member of the AA, and after fucking around under the bonnet, Sable decided to leave the Polo on the hard shoulder. Add to that it was worth less than my suit.

We hatched a plan to hitch a lift; Sable stood with her thumb and tits out while Chris and I hid behind a young sapling. Luckily within five minutes white van man had stopped. His face was a picture when Sable opened the door and jumped in, followed by the rest of Culture Club.

By the time we got dropped off at the bus station, and Sable had phoned a garage, it was approaching 7.30 pm. As luck would have it, the National Express to Luton Airport was just departing. We piled up a few stairs to a few stares and rode the bus back to Luton. Then it was straight into a cab and a dash for the big bash.

Although it was 8.50 pm by now, it was still light as we made our now infamous entry. We strolled across the football pitch towards the stage and a large marquee in full view of the 400 or so colleagues and guests.

Jack Hoben, aka the Grinder, was the first to spot us and announced loudly, "Look here comes Sharky, sorry Sable, with Dumb and Dumber."

Sable lapped it up, as cheers and applause began. He adjusted his pillbox hat and picked his tights out of his arse. Chris and I hung back to give him his big entrance. As he approached the first table comments like "look at you", "she's beautiful" and "well done, so brave" rang out.

"Blimey they've changed their tune." I thought. The wine must certainly have been flowing. Chris and I also milked the applause, like two gladiators returning the queen to the throne, Freddie Mercury would have approved. Then disaster. Someone shouted, "Fucking freak, put the munter down."

Horror, shock, gasp. Sable, taken aback, suddenly turned into a Dick Emery character and tripped on his stilettos, catapulting himself into the nearest table, grabbing the tablecloth in the process. This started a chain reaction as several women were scythed down from their deck chairs. Potato salad cluster bombs exploded, and countless bottles of Chardonnay leapt like lemmings from the table.

Oh shit. . . The disco even paused. Chris and I stood transfixed as we surveyed the damage. A big pile of linen, broken chairs, crockery, glass, garlic dip and kicking legs with assorted knickers lay strewn before us, in other words, a complete train wreck. Others guests rushed in frantically, digging into the pile as if looking for earthquake victims.

I turned to Chris, and we dissolved into tearful fits of laughter. Fuck, was this for real? Surely, It must have been staged?

"I bet that fucker Beadle is behind the ice cream van." I thought.

The Chaos lasted a good thirty minutes until order was restored, but Sable's day, dress, and pride had been badly torn. I'm not sure if his face was filled more with embarrassment or coleslaw, but he had become a raging she-devil. Hey, perhaps Christina was right after all! The women and a fat bloke from St John's rallied round, and he was rushed off to the toilet. Which one? I don't know!

The abuse hurling culprit? Well, he was never caught. Chris and I then made a beeline for the bar and got stuck into free Lowenbrau. We then entertained our fellow workers with tales of the day from marriage to mechanics. Rumour has it Sable went back to a hotel with Sandy the shuffler and was gashed, but I can't verify this, I was too lashed.

And a Funnel

Greece is the word! Well, at least that's what Frank the travel shop advisor said back in '82 when somehow he persuaded me and my mate, Dave, not to venture to Honk Kong but instead book, as he described, a new revolutionary holiday entitled Club 18-30's.

He finished his pitch by assuring us it came with a guaranteed shag and endless booze.

"Yeah sounds great," I said, "Where's that then mate?"

"Spetsai Island, Greece," he replied. "It's going to be the new Magaluf."

You cunt Frank. It turned out to be so small; Robinson Crusoe had to send Friday to Crete every time the tide came in.

All the visions we had been flogged, of sun-kissed golden beaches packed with voluptuous topless maidens feeding us grapes drenched in Metaxa, were total bollocks; this place was less exciting than a school trip to a chartered accountant convention.

It took twelve arduous hours by Desperate Danair-ways, a crummy charabanc, and a flea bitten ferry to reach the promised land. Our luxury villa turned out to be the Acrap-olis, a modern ruin with no swimming pool.

Admittedly we did see the Corinthian Pass, the baby brother of the Panama and Suez canals on our journey, but come on! A whole day gazing at grazing goats, and endless olive trees. The bus had no air con, and it was about 120 degrees.

Oh, how I longed for a pint and a paw paw tree. The first to quench my thirst and the second to scratch my arse like Baloo in Jungle book. This trip was already becoming the holiday from Helios.

The bus was full of wavering wankers looking for Shirley Valentine romances. Incidentally, in the movie the character Shirley sympathetically tells an English couple, "Don't worry about the Mediterranean food Chuck, I'll cook ya some nice chips and egg."

STOP right now! That's the whole fucking point of going abroad, and its egg 'n chips you twat, go and get an education with Rita.

We managed to swap our room to an adjacent building that at least had a fridge, although the next day we found that two size twenty characters from Viz had removed our food and drink. We took our revenge by putting a dead goat's head in their dehydrator.

For some reason, they didn't talk to us for the rest of the holiday, even though we tried are best to use another guest for a scapegoat.

Then every morning at half past 6 am we were awoken by Kojak calling his victims to pray at the Orthodox Church. It sounded similar to a mosque calling, but with added thrash metal bouzoukis. After three days, we had had enough. So one dawn, I launched my flip flop assault, Abo style.

With the golden shot of the century, I skimmed it from our balcony straight through a narrow opening in the spire. It had the desired effect; the Byzantine baller was cut off in mid-wail. I accompanied it with a shout of "Who Loves Ya Baby?"

Yes, I know we should respect other cultures. But we hadn't laid out £450, (which is about half a million in today's money) to be awoken before we had even gone to bed.

Our Buddy group numbered about 25 in total. In truth, they had also been conned into visiting this lifeless place and were reminiscent of the type of people you get on work related bonding weekends. Hardly sex, drugs and rock 'n roll.

For us, this was the most disappointing aspect of our holiday. The birds were a million miles away from Aphrodite and her nymphomaniac mates that we had been promised by Thomas Cook.

On revealing our plight to the Rep, she countering with. "Well, maybe you should have gone to Kowloon then."

"A bit late now." I said, "I wanna a shag, not a suit!"

"You're not my type," she sarcastically quipped.

We soon found names for the cast of our Greek tragedy, which included three mid 40 somethings who must have forged their passports.

We had Charles Fat lass, the flabby-chested, camp mustachioed bodybuilder, (the original Schwarzenegger) who had more Brussels than mussels; Next there was Puff one, and Puff two, the first being a pasty pastry-faced hippie who was chicken and magic mushroom. Puff two, a.k.a. Pissed-up Floater, was a guy who would gradually inflate with alcohol and turn into a lilo, drifting around the Aegean all day.

We also had the disappointment in the form of five lads from Bridgend, who pissed out the window and filled up their granny's sombrero. Think they only had one party song.

The youngest member of our group was a schizo, called Steve, a 19-year-old manic-depressive from Bognor Regis, who's answer to every activity was. "That's fleas' piss, man," or "This Greek beer is gnats' piss, man."

In the end, I told him, "Shut the fuck up, you're pissing me off, man."

The females consisted of Charlie's Mingers, a blond, a brunette, and a bowl head from Essex. Then we had the Stepford sisters, two androids on roller skates, whose highlight of the day was which cereal to choose from the variety pack. Then last and nearly least, six nurses all called plain Jane from St. Elsewhere.

Oh, sorry, I forgot Sharon and Tracy from Geordieshire or Shore, or Biker Grove as it was known by then.

Dave and I had desperately tried to get on with the Fat Slags and the rest of the girls, but they had collectively already decided long ago, probably on our laborious coach journey that we were reprobates. Maybe they had a slight point but, 'hey' they were hardly Hot Gossip.

At the BBQ night, things were rocking, and as the Seven-Up flowed, Spiros the waiter, who claimed to be 108 years old delivered 28 lamb dishes, as nobody dare order Turkey. The Demis Roussos tribute band. Jason and the Argonauts were in fine Feta and had everybody swaying with their AEK lighters.

The conversation was also riveting, as the table discussed Latin at school. Dave and I were so bored we opened a tin of Dulux then watched to see what would happen. Suddenly an unexpected sympathetic invitation was tossed in our direction when one of the Sisters of Mercy, Jane, asked us if we would like to inject some life and soul.

So we did, with Animal House-style party games. Unfortunately, I think they had pin the tail on the donkey in mind, not the Trojan War.

Beware of false chavs bearing gifts! Our offer to serve our table dinner quickly turned from lemon juggling into a full-on food fight. We put up a great battle, but by their sheer numbers and aided by 300 Spartans, Muller light and egg plant, we were eventually, repelled to the doghouse.

We stood and watched the entertainment from the safety

of the bar, twenty metres from our foes. We then decide to trade in our ouzo and purchase a bottle of Retsina. In retrospect, an unwise choice.

We cracked it open and happily shared it with old Spiros while his family invited holidaymakers up to smash plates and do a bit of 3000BC line dancing.

Poor old Spiros nearly didn't make it to 109, when, by mistake, we smashed a real soup terrine over his head. The end of the night deteriorated, culminating into a debauchery of underwater nude Greco wrestling. This was to be the final nail in our character assassination, and we were annexed from our group for the rest of the vacation as total slop suckers.

The next day it was absolutely roasting, so we thought we'd give the beach a miss. We decided to hire out mopeds for the day and do a tour of the Island. Unfortunately, my partner in crime, big Dave, almost broke his neck when our tour turned into the Isle of Spetsai Moto GP.

We had started off sedately enough but as the Spetsai had a circumference smaller than Dave's bellend we decided we would race round it ten times to get our money's worth.

By lap five, I felt a bit sorry for Dave. He was a big old boy and with our racing machines only sporting Qualcast engines, it meant he, not the motor, was pushing his bike up every incline in 120 degrees.

Then disaster, as he leapt on his machine at the top of Spiros Mirabeau, he suddenly lost the back end and slammed down the hill into Foghorn Leghorn. He was promptly arrested for dangerous driving and killing the champion village rooster.

After three hours in the police station, they eventually returned his passport after he paid them a golden fleece for foul play. The bike was a write-off, but more worryingly, so was Dave's leg.

Every day after that Dave invalided himself to the yachting club, where he drunk himself into a stupor and stuffed himself in the style of Cool Hand Luke with boiled eggs and olives from the very limited menu.

After a couple more days, he became withdrawn, a recluse, hiding himself away like a shipping magnate, while I windsurfed into my own Exxon Valdez.

Then, two days before we were due to go home, Dave announced to me that he was dying of gangrene, and he desperately needed to exercise his infected leg and see a quack. I fully endorsed this plan and built him a crutch from an old parasol, Socrates sandal and a dog's bone, (a good scout never leaves his man). The next morning I helped Dave to dress in his stripey t-shirt and party headwear. Dave had an Admiral's hat and me a blue Pixie number with a little bell.

With helping arm, we Jake the Pegged off to see Dr Spiros, the local physician, who cleaned and re-bandaged his leg, but told Dave he needed to get to a hospital. He also gave him antibiotics that Dave immediately threw away.

"Fuck that, I'm not giving up drinking, I'm on holiday" he adamantly announced.

We set off again for the harbour, where we knew an independent disco boat set off every day for a six-hour jolly. I told Dave that if he dipped his leg into the sea the salt might help cleanse his wounds.

"Yeah, or free lunch for a shark." He remarked.

We made the harbour eventually and purchased two tickets for 3000 Drachmas, that's around £5 each, from Spiros tours, the ticket vendor. He informed us in Greeklish the boat was called the Spirit of Spiros.

"No kidding mate, everyone or thing on this island is called fucking Spiros." I said, obviously.

He told Dave the boat was painted red and white.

"You have a funnel please, OK, and don't drinking too much guys."

"Yeah mate, cheers," we replied.

We headed off down to the quay; we looked around, but I couldn't see any red and white boat, just a small blue ferry, a few cruisers, and the modest Spetsai fishing fleet.

Suddenly Dave fell off his perch.

"There it is, Si. . . And it's going. Quick, get my crutch."

We hobbled down as fast as we could, and I called out to the boat some excellent Greek along the lines of excusey Capitan, Basta, Basta! But the people just stared back at me with blank expressions. Not being defeated by this, I took on Bob Beamon's record and leapt on, and somehow clawed myself up.

Dave looked at me all dejected like a salty sea-dog left shipwrecked.

"Don't worry, X marks the spot." I shouted.

"Yer What?"

"I'll get you as we come astern."

The boat slipped passed the next jetty then turned back starboard towards Dave, I reached out to him and dragged him by the crotch and his crutch, and bundled him aboard.

Fuck me, that was hard work, especially in that heat. We finally took up a position right at the back of the boat, as Dave was in a lot of pain.

"Don't look much like a disco boat to me." I said, looking round.

Everybody was looking religious in black, and they were all women.

"Ah, they're probably just locals cadging a lift to Kos." Said Dave. "Italians, Greeks, and Spanish, they all wear black once they hit 40."

"Why's that then?" I asked. Nun the wiser!

After reaching a speed of about ten knots. Equal to ten minutes of wave chugging, we decided to explore the boat as not much seemed to be happening downstairs, and besides where were all the other mugs who had paid 1500 Dracula's?

I helped Dave up, and we climbed untidily up a small flight of wooden steps and hopped onto the main deck.

"Ahoy there!" We shouted. But then froze, flabbergasted, as a funeral ceremony was in full flow.

There was an open coffin in the centre of the boat, which was resting on a table. It was garnished with Olympic style laurel leaves, bouquets of Taramasalata, and Feta cheese plants, or maybe that was the buffet. Fifty or so sombre guests gathered round the deck listening to a priest giving his dearly departed sermon. We tried to hide in the galley, but to say we looked out of place was an understatement. The mourners repeatedly stared at Noddy and Captain Hook as we cringed in the Galley.

"Oh fuck." We said in unison.

One of the ministers came towards us and put his fingers to his mouth and signalled for us to sit down. The main pope geezer started swinging a smoking pot, and then the mourners took it in turn to lob single flowers over the side. A few prayers were said out loud as the coffin was closed and manhandled onto a slide and bumped down into the azure waters.

It started to sink; I looked at Dave, we didn't know whether to salute or swim for it. I moved towards the back of the boat and turned to Dave and beckoned him to retrace our steps. He started to struggle towards the stairs but his leg was weeping louder than the mourners, so he gave up and sat on a buoy.

"Sorry mate, didn't see you there."

One of the funeral party then came over asked us something in Greek. I suppose it was something along the lines of "What the hell are you doing here?"

All we could do was hold up our hands and shrug.

Dave then utilsed his grasp of the language and said, "Sorry mate, mistakio, mistakio."

The woman was expressionless.

I said, "Dave this is Greece, it's no good talking Spanish."

"Oh yeah, sorry mate. er mousaka mousaka."

The old woman tutted and gave a sigh, then walked off. Next the priest appeared and asked again in Greek something like. "Do you normally attend funerals in fancy dress."

I took over the cultural attache role and replied in slow motion with extended hand gestures.

"Yes, we are very . . . very . . . S.o.r.r.y. yer Grace, b.u.t, we get-ting on wrong boatio, we look-ing for Dis Co Bowt."

He cut me off. "OK, so you are English, and you made a mistake. Why doesn't that surprise me? Please stay quiet and take a seat. We're going back now, and please remember to respect people's privacy."

"Of course your majesty, no problem." Assured a grovelling Dave.

"Oh, and sorry about the flip-flop." I added.

We sat there in the blazing heat not daring to move, and then a bent old nun, probably next in line for the water chute, offered us a fish head kebab and a glass of ouzo.

"Efcharistó." (thank you). Rude to not accept I thought.

We tucked in and almost immediately retched, but nodded in polite appreciation.

"This is fuffing wevoltin." Dave said from the side of his mouth.

"Just keep snyling mate." I said through gritted teeth.

After twenty minutes, we reached the jetty and hastily gobbed two fish balls over the side. They were quickly cannibalised by Costas the Catfish. After embarking onto dry land, we turned and repeatedly bowed all apologetic like.

"Right, let's get a refund." Said Dave.

From the top of the climb, we noticed the real disco boat anchored about 1500 yards out to sea. We could hear Zorba the Greek pumping out and also hear the cheers of the bikini-clad models participating in party games.

Spiros the Vendor was akip when we arrived outside his ticket box.

We woke him up with a thunderous bang on his glass.

"Woz up you?" He said, startled. "Woz the problem, Uh?"

"The Disco disco boat mate, that's the problem," said Dave.

"Iz no finish! Why, and how do you come back?" He asked, scratching his nuts.

"Yeah, we know that. You sent us on the wrong boat Spiros!"

"No, no, no, you go wrong boat, Mr." Argued Spiros.

"Yes Mr, because you told us WRONG BOAT. You said the boat with a red funnel, you fuckwit." Said Dave, becoming a bit annoyed.

"What you talk like, uh?" Replied Spiros.

He thought for a minute then started to laugh.

"OK, big man. Now I tell you. You to go have fun ah, not talk this funnel." He laughed again.

"What is funnel?" He then asked.

"Very fucking funny mate," said Dave.

"Listen, Spiros, we ended up on a floating crem! Comprehendo?

"I limped three fucking miles to hop aboard a tug where I scraped my arse on a buoy and chewed a fish head with a dead bloke I've never even met. The boat had no fucking beer, no music and less atmosphere than Jupiter. So if you wanna keep your St George's cross, you better give my 3000 Drachmas back, NOW."

Dave then grabbed him by the ears and hauled him over the counter.

"OK ,OK, You get big trouble now!" Shouted Spiros as he threw the money from his pocket on the counter, he then gave us his best piercing look and preceded to slam the hatch down.

I whispered in Dave's ear. "We'd better do the offski before he calls his brothers, all 900 of them! Plus it was Malta."

"What was? Said Dave

"The George Cross thing."

"Don't matter", he said, "Same fucking island, different flag."

Spiros opened the glass up again and started hurling Greek insults down the road at us.

"What do you think he's saying Dave?" I asked, just for entertainment value.

"Dunno." He randomly opened his phrase book up and laughed.

"What, what?"

He began reading, "Hóverkráft mu íne gemáto hélia."

"My hovercraft is full of eels!"

The last day we decided to get a hydrofoil to Piraeus, the port of Athens, as it only took 4 hours. We planned to meet up with my brother because the cruise ship *ss Oriana* was in town, at the time one of P&O's largest liners. We had arrived three hours before the ship docked, so we decided to get Dave's leg redressed.

We found a surgery, but it was closed. I went to a pharmacy and became Florence Nightingale for the morning.

We found a bar. It was tiny, so we had to lean outside to keep Dave's leg straight. We noticed across the road there was a huge queue of sailors waiting to get into enormous decaying building. On further inspection we realised it was some kind of cinema, so we thought, we'll have some of that, if only to pass the time. We joined the queue with 200 multi-national seamen. I had noticed earlier that the port was full of a whole host of vessels. After twenty minutes, we finally reached the foyer.

"Five hundred each," I informed Dave after noticing the tariff board.

"What's the movie guv? And is it subtitled?" I asked the man at the door.

He just gave me a toothless grin and waved us through.

"I reckon it's First Blood," I said.

Dave guessed Star Trek's latest offering. We ambled through the foyer; Dave's leg was starting to heal slowly but looked bad as his bandage was soaked bright red from all the iodine.

My hand had also turned bright yellow from the antiseptic I had rubbed on. Dave renamed me Fluorescent Nightingale! He had taken most of his smarties of antibiotics and pain killers because we knew this was a gonna be a big session with the crew of the Oriana. Although probably unadvisable, the drugs enabled him to walk almost normally.

As we waited for our Pepsi, customers kept coming and going. I opened the curtain to find some old hag giving most of the crew of HMS Philippines a blowjob.

"Oh, excuse me." I said, slightly confused.

Dave opened the next one, same thing, fucking strange cinema, don't think the Odeon would approve I thought.

We followed the torch bearing usher into a humungous cinema, but there were no seats, just standing room, it was stifling. About a thousand ancient mariners were shuffling on a huge terrace as Linda Lovelace's mouth, projected in gigantic resolution, did her best in Deep Throat.

The hanging air was overripe, body odour mixed with seamen's' semen and cheap Russian cigarettes had us gagging.

We decided to leave Linda to blow the sixth fleet and

headed straight for the exit but somehow became fair game for the crew of SS Gaylord. They followed us out. The big mother at the front was chewing a cigar and encouraged his mates to join him as the Benny Hill chase began.

We weaved through a maze of alleys and squares, fuck they were gaining on us. As Dave's leg began to falter, we turned into a big square and found sanctuary in a church.

"What the fuck was that all about?" Said, Dave.

"Dunno but Bob Todd had the hots for you."

"Can we claim diplomatic immunity?" Said Dave.

"Well we'll find out soon," I said, "here comes yet another priest and he's got his cassock in a twist."

"Taxiiii", said Dave, loudly.

We slipped out of a side door, I checked, all clear. After 15 minutes of being totally lost which lasted half an hour, we found the main road and grabbed a horse and chariot.

The Oriana was already berthed when we arrived. The taxi driver, obviously a U2 fan, wouldn't take our money and kept pointing to his watch and repeating "Sunday, Bloody Sunday." Oh you mean double Neddy?"

We ambled along the quayside and hopped onto the gang-plank, as security was lapse in those days, so we just strolled on board.

We then asked a hairdresser if she knew my brother, Graham.

THE SEARCH FOR THE GOOSE'S PALM

Within ten minutes he arrived. He took Dave swiftly to see the ships doctor while I went to the Pig (the crew bar) and sampled several subsidised pale ales and duty-free Dunhill.

After a couple of hours on the piss, a bloke called big Jack from Barnsley and Halifax, from Sheffield, not Halifax, decided to join us, plus a bloke called Desperate from darkest Cornwall and a posse of deck hands. We went and grabbed Dave.

It was time to hit Athens and have a night on the town. Most of it is a blur now, but I do remember tucking into the biggest Olympic size pizza I'd ever seen served on a dustbin lid.

I also have vague recollections of the Aristotle club and the taxi ride home. We were pretty much legless from 6 pm, especially Dave!

The next morning I awoke on the floor and crawled into the bathroom and accidentally smashed a small statue on the shelf.

"Fuck I've broken its head off." I said to Dave.

"Don't worry, I think it's meant to be like that." He said.

Dave was already packed. "Hurry up, we have a plane to catch," he moaned.

Ten minutes later we set off for the airport, but I had to go back to the hotel because I'd forgotten some trivial things like my passport and wallet.

Dave arrived and went to the airport bar where he received a cold beer and cold shoulder from our fellow group, who by now had become a tight unit.

I arrived extremely late, and after rushing through their impressive security, i.e., some bloke smoking a fag and scratching his arse, I sprinted through the boarding gate.

I joined the queue at the bottom of the aircraft steps.

"Nice holiday?" I asked one of the Stepford Sisters.

"Yeah, after you's went, 10/10." She said, nastily.

"Oh, thanks very much," I said. "I'd only give it 18 out of 30."

CHAPTER 8

Jungle Rock

"Welcome to Banjul international airport," said the flight attendant, "Where the local time is 3 pm. Please remember not to adjust your watches as Gambia is on GMT. The temperature is 31 degrees celsius and weather at the moment it better than at home. Thank you for flying Air Europe, and we hope to see you again."

"I fucking hope so," I thought, "It's a long walk home."

Banjul International was basically a school desk at the end of a runway with the not so welcoming face of immigration sat behind it. After stamp collecting it was a small stroll down a gated path leading through a football turnstile into a tin shed that doubled as a fish market on Tuesday. I think they only had three international flights a week, not including the Wright On brothers who operated a shuttle to Dakar. The airfield looked deserted, except for a couple of old military wrecks waiting to be put down plus the fire engine from Trumpton.

It all seemed very strange when we landed; the pilot just indicated, and then wheel spun the 767 finishing with a hand brake turn. With looks of trepidation, we clambered down a window cleaners' ladder. The flight time was five and a half hours, so with two crews they never got off. I think they had a fat jerry can of two-star and a puncture repair kit for emergencies. The bags were jettisoned onto wheelbarrows; a flight plan was filed with some bloke up a tree who had a telescope. then they fucked off as quick as they could. Well, they did in 1990.

After identifying our cases, they were then slung on the back of an army truck. We, the intrepid explorers, were herded on tourist coaches that were so old they had square wheels. The driver waved his red flag, and we set off at a crawl to our respective alleged resorts, followed by dozens of cheering, shoeless school kids. I had just split from a long term relationship with my Italian girlfriend, so I felt I needed a break from all the shit that goes with splitting up and the heart-rending moment I gave my espresso machine back, so I decided to lose myself for a week in deepest, darkest Africa.

Gambia is on the West coast of Africa and is the smallest country on the continent. It has a tiny stretch of Atlantic coast and clings to a wiggly river that forms the filling for a Senegalese sandwich. English is mainly spoken, as it was a British colony until 1965 and although I knew it would hardly be Dr Livingstone territory, the darkest was in reference to its mystique, not as I found out later, to its daily power cuts. The country is very poor and was controlled by some tin-pot regime as per the norm, claiming to be democratic.

Driving through the villages on mud roads, you got the impression their GDP was on a level with a game of shove ha'penny, as back then the word tourism had just been added to their dictionary, just below torture. Although, there were signs of investment and infrastructure to be seen, signs like the one supplied by Coca-Cola, who had arrived with a light box and stuck it outside Kentucky Fried Gibbon. The natives were inquisitive but also slightly restless, and who wouldn't be? Watching rich white tourists chug past your mud hut must have seemed like watching a limping wildebeest to a pride of lions.

We arrived at our hotel, the Atlantis, about a three star with five-star prices. I had prepared myself for this from experience, as most things except the insects would have been imported. My room was the part in black and white decor plus a few shields and spears slung on the walls. The rooms centrepiece was decaying stuffed attack squirrel over my bed, but there were few mod cons and no TV. Mind you, I wasn't that bothered, I'd already seen King Solomon's Mines around grandmas. The air con kind of worked if you beat it to within an inch of its life, and there was an empty fridge with a welcoming film of mould.

By the bed were two books, the Bible and Cooking for Cannibals. The recipe for spotted dick looked nice. French sounding snacks lay on a coffee table nestled in a shallow basket, half covering hotel literature of a local hedge-hopping map. The bathroom had Gulliver's bath, but a Lilliputian shower and no door or view with the windows heavily fortified, which gave you the feeling of imprisonment, and that they were trying to keep more than mosquitoes out.

The resort bore a resemblance to the village in Daktari, well that's what I thought. It was set amongst an acre of tropical gardens. I recognised some of the fauna from Amsterdam coffee shops. There were also several palm trees by the nicely shaped pool. The reception was a two story building plastered with pictures of President Jawara and one of Jimmy Carter, probably due to his peanut affiliation. There was a sparsely filled souvenir shop with racks of I love Gambia pens and an equipment-less fitness centre with a picture of Peter Shilton pulling a Bullworker. Oh, and President Jawara winning the Banjul marathon in a Harry Enfield shellsuit.

I decided this was all acceptable as I was in Africa not Albufeira, and just being in Africa was pretty cool. They had two bars, one by the pool and one in the restaurant/entertainment area, which backed onto the large beach that stretched out about 800 metres in either direction. It was a dirty, not golden, brown. A cunning trick you often find in holiday brochures, like the ocean, which was a greyish, not turquoise, blue. Again I figured they were using shots of the Bahamas or a turquoise filter. However, it did have proper waves, and it was surprisingly bloody cold.

The first day it took me the standard 30 minutes to wade in over my waist like a big Jesse, although I did fall in a panic when I stood on the highly dangerous stone fish that turned out to be a stone in the shape of a fish. I waded some more, but I could soon feel rips and as there were no lifeguards within 2,000 miles and Jaws was looking for his lunch, I decided to stay at the pool for the rest of the day, listening to The Sea by The Cure on my Walkman.

The power cuts were a pain but hey, when in Rome. They did have generators, but not much fuel. The main problem for dining by candlelight was that after some while my bottled beer started to warm up. I can't remember the name, something like Jutbrew. It had the token elephant on the front and was about 8% in strength which made it almost undrinkable when not frozen like a jubbly. They even had a pilsner at 10% called Cobra. Probably more deadly than the real thing. I thought the moon lit evenings gave the place a more romantic and slightly frontier feel, like being back in the days of a largely undiscovered continent. . . Any minute now we would be attacked, like in Zulu. I couldn't make up my mind if I were to play Michael Caine or Stanley Baker; I noticed a real minister dining in the restaurant. 'Mr. Witt! When I have the impertinence to climb into your pulpit to deliver a sermon, then you can tell me my duty'.

The attack never came, but I did do a karaoke version of *Men of Harlech* when the band turned up. Some of the guests still thought they were in Torremolinos and complained like whinging poms (as one lone token Aussie liked to remind me). But he was bang on. What is it about the Brits abroad? Our reputation in tatters. From the once mighty British empire, built by kings, queens, admirals and generals over 300 years to be destroyed in 300 beers by football hooligans and Mr and Mrs Grumbleweed.

Africa doesn't have Holland's meat and potato pies, the Sunday People or Johns Smith bitter. Get over it. Who fucking cares if Sheffield Wednesday beat Leeds, as some oink kept shouting down reception's lone telephone. "Can ya hear me? It's Brian, you know Brian. I'm int Gambia. Gam-bee-yar, you know, Africa. Near Teneriffe. Remember movie out of Africa? You what? Nay, I've not left yet. Look, what's Leeds score lad?"

"Is everything OK sir?" Enquired the receptionist.

"No, it ain't. We bloody lost two nil. . . and get some bloody decent phones. It's '90s now lass.

"No, it's Africa." I thought. "Yorkshire is not a superpower, you fuckwit."

The guests were a cross section of Liquorish Allsorts. Oh yeah, and a few old oil men who never went home from test drilling in the '70s. I teamed up with a bloke from Edmonton called Chris. Mainly because he was being hunted by a couple of tasty females, Sam and Sarah, who were freelance journalists with a then newish news channel called Sky. On the second day, there was breaking news on the jungle drums. Margaret Thatcher had resigned, which had them scrambling to B.I.A., and throwing cash at anyone with a pilot's license but with no luck. They were last seen heading into the sunset aboard the African Queen with Humphrey Bogart. They are probably still on it. 'Play it again Sam' said, Sarah.

The day trips were the usual rubbish you get when tourism is in its infancy. Examples included a trip to see Charley the man-eating 12-inch crocodile or Mr Tomba's game safari, with a guest appearance from the local Johnny Morris. Hardly animal magic mate, unless you count trying to spot the lesser spotted trotter bird. Now that was a game. Fort Bullen, an old British outpost once used for slavery sounded interesting, but three stone blocks and a rusting canon in the sand was hardly Windsor Castle. Plenty of village tours, where on offer was an opportunity to sample life as it may have been, or still was. The highlight was going to see the witch doctor and have your life story told through the medium of bovine entails. Always ending with, "My friend, good luck will come to you and your family if you cross my palm with dalasi (money)."

If no palm crossing took place, historically, the doc would often put a curse on your wife's goat. Go ahead son, I hated my mother-in-law. The schools were worth a visit, as the kids seemed in general happy with very little, and many tourists brought gifts of pens, books and sweets with them. I took a box of crayons and six Cadbury's creme eggs, which in the heat turned into a Madame Tussauds omelette. Let's see you do that Jamie.

After Chris's chicks had suddenly headed home, we were at a bit of a loss. Until one night, we were invited by a French fish buyer named Andre, out for a meal at one of Gambia's more exclusive fodder houses. Not sure why, but probably because we'd plied him with Ricard the night before. He arranged a jeep to pick us up at dusk. Off we set with Kinga, who we renamed

Klinger, our driver and guide. As we headed further into the bush, we were repeatedly stopped by the plod who loved to shine torches in our eyes and on our shoes.

"Do you have any i.d.?"

"Err, no."

"Well, give me your pens."

Chris did have a Tottenham ballpoint that he handed over, but they wanted Man. Utd. We arrived at another hotel.

"Is this it?" I asked Klinger.

"No sir, this is the hotel Reef. We are meeting up with Mr Andre for a drink first.

"OK, wait here corporal," I said, "Here's five bucks for a new dress."

We parked up, and Chris and I spotted Andre at the pool bar. It was the standard straw circular hut design and very busy. We shook hands and ordered beer. Everybody knew Andre; it was like a UN jolly. I started to stare at this big black guy next to me's arm, as it had a giant scar running all the way from his shoulder to his hand, like a tattoo of a huge serpent. He looked down at me.

"Shark bite?" I enquired.

He laughed. "No, my brother did it."

"Nice guy." I remarked.

"He slept with my wife," said his brother, another huge man.

They both laughed. You see, he has four wives already, and he was getting greedy. They seemed very jovial about a serious domestic. I started chatting with them and bought them a beer. They were from Liberia and were working with the Gambian peacekeeping force. It crossed my mind that maybe their CV wasn't ideally compatible with peace.

Gambia is predominately a Muslim country, but the bit about not drinking alcohol in the Koran must have been torn out. These boys were on Johnnie Walker Black chasers. Andre called over that it was time to go, We said our good-byes and climbed aboard the jeep . Fifteen minutes of night safari brought us to a clearing where there was a slightly run-down looking restaurant with a customary partly lit neon sign. Couldn't help thinking, even in those days that perhaps "Lard" wasn't the best name for a restaurant.

There were armed security guards outside in combat fatigues but no shoes. Was there sanctions in place on footwear I didn't know about? I must send Dr Marten a letter. Andre beckoned us, and we strolled through the front door. Once inside I must admit it was very swanky, considering we were in Tarzan's back garden. It was awash with French memorabilia, artists impressions of Giant Paris landmarks covered the walls, but the mini Eiffel Tower lamps on each table made it a little bit over fromage-y for me.

Andre introduced us to his Wife, Claudia, and the chef and proprietor Maurice. He was from Provence, and his food was top notch. He also had decent bottles of Sancerre and ice-cold Heineken. Sitting contently in La Jardin after being fed and watered, with XO in hand, Andre, Claudia Chris and I were joined at our table by a couple of local young, fit, well dressed local jars of honey. They sparkled in their sequins and must have been in their early twenties. We were informed that they were the daughters of general Motobo, Ninti and Sherri, who had been partly educated in Surrey at a private school. They spoke with eloquence and intelligence about England and their love of London shopping. Chris's chat about The Spurs was starting to wear rather thin. Amazingly, the girls seemed uninterested in the subject of was Hoddle better than Platini? Going for the sympathy vote, I decided to intervene with sorry tales of my recent separation.

"Where in Italy did you say your partner came from?" Slurred Claudia.

"Ex-partner." I said promptly "and Napoli, that's Naples, Chris."

"I know the geezer, we beat em 1-0 in 1979." He said, confidently.

I lit up a Benson. "Oh she was a moolie then," said Claudia.

"Sorry, a what?"

"Um, you say she was a nigger."

Utter silence.

I dropped my Zippo lighter into the brandy while wondering if she had a death wish. She continued, "See, that's what we call people from the South of Italy, no offence ladies, but that's where blacks and the peasants come from."

"And the mafia," I thought.

I remembered going to Italia '90 in July for the World Cup, where I watched England beat Cameroon in Naples and the local vendors all complaining that the North of the country treated them like shit. Meanwhile, I weighed up whether she had a death wish or was Mussolini's granddaughter.

Andre said something in Italian which I think roughly translated to "Are are you fucking mad? Speaking like that in front of the daughters of Gambia's Idi Amin!"

She gave him the finger, stood up, St Moritz and Martini in hand and sloped off.

The general's daughters expressions transformed from insulted to infuriated, as they ripped off their expensive Dior numbers to reveal Mandela United tracksuits and fired up their Bridgestones.

After careful consideration of the situation now rapidly developing I thought "oh fuck."

Andre began unreservedly apologising for his wife's offensive remarks, but Chris, oblivious to the situation, jumped in and did his best to inflame the situation with come on's and a story about how he was partial to a bit of ebony punani. Andre nearly choked again tried to rescue the evening by fumbling pictures from his wallet of his new puppy, Benson, but you could tell that the girls weren't interested in shagging dog stories.

Andre ordered some coffee. "Ladies, please accept my apologies. Claudia is drunk."

The girls graciously accepted Andre's apology, but the atmosphere still felt uncomfortable. Then chef Maurice decided to join us at the table. He pulled up a chair and melted.

Just then the door opened and in marched the army's top brass. My arsehole tightened, and I half closed my eyes. This was it. John Simpson was soon gonna be reporting on my untimely death.

"Hello daddy." Said the girls, as the general walked to our table.

He was a huge man; even Jackamo don't make his size. Chewing on a big cigar, he was wearing a full metal jacket, but this one was sagging with medals Kenny Everett style. His Hennessey arrived.

"Would you like something to eat general?" Offered Maurice.

"No thank you, Maurice, I'm watching my waistline."

He was also watching me, so I looked at Notre dame.

"I've come to collect the girls."

He then took a lungful of his Havana and looked me up and down again.

"And you are?"

"Err, I'm nobody important. . . Just a holidaymaker." I squeaked, like Shaggy meeting a ghost in Scooby Doo.

"What is your name?"

"Simon. . . sir."

"Tell me, Simon, why are you looking nervous boy? We don't eat tourists."

He then looked at Chris, who semi saluted and then uttered a famous African greeting.

"Evening guvnor, what's up?"

I grimaced.

"Are you two brothers?"

"No." I interrupted, "We met chasing after two girls in our hotel. Then they had to leave because the iron lady resigned, on a boat.

Trying to make sense of my waffling he said. "Are you are saying Margaret Thatcher has resigned?"

I nodded in affirmation.

"You know," he said, "Our president is a very good friend of she and of great Britain. In fact, he was at Prince Charles' wedding. Well, half of it."

The other officers laughed on cue like they do in movies. I wondered if I was missing the punchline. I found out later he had returned to crush a coup d'état.

"So you are from England?"

"Yes mate, London." Said Chris,

"I'm from Luton; that's near London." I said.

The general looked up to the ceiling and blew a slow, lazy smoke ring while he thought about my answer.

"Luton. That's near the elephant and castle. I think a bus goes there."

"Several." I said.

"I do like London though, especially when it snows. But not my wife. She and my daughters prefer to enjoy themselves with my credit card at Harrods."

The girls gave him a scornful look.

"Yes, I like to stay at Claridges or the Dorchester. They have good soap and some fine cognacs."

He laughed again and said, "Unlike this one."

With that he downed the contents of his glass, stood up and told the girls they had to go as he had some work to do.

"Goodnight general, nice to see you." Fawned Andre.

Maurice accompanied C brigade to the door as well as Ninti and Sherri. Sherri turned to Andre and then glared at Claudia in the corner.

She advised Andre to "ditch da bitch."

The general looked at them puzzled, but carried on out of the door.

We breathed a sigh of relief as it closed. Shit, that was uncomfortable to say the least. We slumped at the table as outside the convoy left in three jeeps and the customary "dictators r us" old black Merc.

The restaurant was now empty of patrons except for me and Chris.

Andre headed straight for Miss Scarlett.

"Murder in the kitchen with a candlestick." I said.

Chris said "Typical Juventus," and then pointed his eyebrows to the door.

We swiftly fucked off as the battle of Banjul broke out,

Maurice acted like nothing was happening and started to cash up as we eased ourselves out of the front door,

"Hey Chris, we didn't pay the bill." I said.

"Don't worry, we'll sort it later. . ."

"Oi, where's Klinger gone?"

"Fuck knows," said Chris. "Come on, we'll flag a taxi down."

"A taxi! Out here?"

After walking for an hour down a dusty track I announced that it was a fucking stupid idea as we are in the middle of nowhere, it's the middle of the night, and we are being tracked down by Masai tribesmen and a big cat called Clarence.

"Don't worry, they're both in Kenya." Said Chris.

"So will we be soon."

Just then a car pulled up. "Hooray, its a black cab." Chris cheered.

We couldn't see for the headlights who was inside, then out stepped two coppers.

"This gets fucking better and better." I thought.

"Get in the car." requested the tall one.

"You what?" said Chris.

"In the car." Ordered the short one, pointing his Wyatt Earp pistol.

We sat in silence as my Creme Brulee worked its way down. We then came to a small village and pulled up by an illuminated shack which had Ganga Rock police station hand painted on a plank nailed to the wall.

We got out of our decaying red and white 1970's Peugeot, which had Banjul fire service on the door. Then followed the police into the station.

I had seen this place before, in an episode of Capetown Cops. I entered with genuine fear. We were led into a small cell, like the ones you get in cowboy films, with see through bars and told to sit on the wooden bench. We were the only "prisoners." I nervously whispered to Chris that it looked like Robben Island for us.

"Naaaaa," he chuffed. "Look, we didn't rob anyone, just forgot the bill."

The alleged police station was sparsely furnished. A lone constable battered out a report on an old typewriter. As I contemplated our situation. Eventually, the constable spoke. "Tell me your names, address, Hotel, nationality, shoe size, etc."

What is it with the shoes? The questions went on for thirty minutes. Just as we finished our story, the big cheese came into the room.

"Good evening," he said. "I am Inspector Dillon Fin-tim-lin-bin-whin-bim-lim bus-stop F'tang-F'tang-Olé Biscuitbarrel Umbugo."

He ripped the sheet from the typewriter, and as he read down the page, he mumbled.

"Mmm ha, mmm ha."

He finished with "Mm nani." Twice. (Which I discovered means no in Mandinka).

"So why didn't you arrange transport back from La Jardin?"

"Well," said Chris, "It's like this, me ol China. We left in a hurry, and our driver bloke had done the offski. I know it was stupid, yeah, we shoulda weighed the bill. But Andres Mrs was right Hampton-wick."

I quickly cut him off trying to explain that were extremely sorry and would pay Maurice tomorrow; it was just a mix-up officer.

Chris, in agreement, said, "See, we fort general Motobo had paid."

Fucking hell Chris, that's almost as bad as Claudia. I thought The inspector's eyes turned into Louis Armstrong hitting a high note on the trumpet.

"You know general Motobo?"

"Know him, we had dinner with him . . . Yeah, he had chicken." Said Chris, laughing.

I gave Chris a hostile glare I normally reserve for unbelievably stupid comments which may result in execution.

"I don't know what you boys are up to," said the inspector. "But I will give you the benefit of the doubt. A car will take you back to your hotel, but make no mistake; I will be watching you. This is not your local park, you don't just go off into the bush on your own, there are many people who could, and would, rob or harm you without thinking twice."

"Sounds just like my park," I thought.

By then it was about 4 am and I just wanted my pit. Next thing I know it's about 11 am and the cleaner, big mamma, was knocking on my door. I pulled some shorts on and opened the door wearing them and thumping hangover.

"Come in, come in."

"I can come back," Mr Simon.

"No, it's OK. I need to get up."

I had made friends with big mama. She seemed a good-hearted sort with a large family and liked to chat with the guests. I sat on the bed arranging my tackle.

"I'll start in the bathroom," Mr Simon.

"Good idea," I thought, reaching for the paracetamol.

Suddenly a scream rang out causing me almost to swallow the bottle. She came scurrying out with the mop at battle stations. I jumped up wondering what was up.

"There's a snake in your boot." She said.

This was pre-Toy Story, so Woody can't sue me for plagiarism. I approached the bathroom on my toes like the cat sneaking past the sleeping dog.

Big Mama said, "I will go get Mr Flavo, you not touch it, OK Mr Simon".

"No chance of that," I thought.

I gingerly peered into the bathroom and there, in my baseball boot, was indeed a thin emerald coloured snake, half asleep with a head like the green triangle in a tin of Quality Street.

"Fucking hell."

It opened one eye and looked at me. So I jumped onto my bed and ripped Tufty of the wall, and lobbed it straight at my boot. I was hoping the snake might think it was a mongoose and leg it, but as snakes haven't got any, it just slithered towards the bath.

Mr Flavo and the gang arrived with a sack and an assortment of sticks, poles and a small pig called Pato.

"Don't worry sir, please come out of your room."

The commotion had attracted a few guests who needed my qualified explanation.

"There's a giant snake in my bed." I said, which caused a bit of alarm.

"I could do with one of those," joked the resident camp tourist as if auditioning for a part in a Carry On film.

"Did it move like a black mamba?" Asked Essex man.

"It's not fucking dancing; it's hungry," I answered.

The door opened and out walked Mr Flavo with a sack held aloft.

"Everything OK now, Mr Simon." He said.

Pato, the pig, trotted out and was looking chuffed. Mr Flavo explained pigs are immune to snake bites. How true this is I still don't know.

"What type of snake is it?" Asked Essex. "Is it a Black Mamba or a Pit Viper?"

"No, no harmless. Just tree snake."

Essex looked disappointed.

"Do you know a lot about snakes, sir?" Asked Mr Flavo.

His wife interrupted. "He bought a book on African reptiles, the nearest he's come to a snake is landing on one in a board game at Christmas."

We all laughed.

"I was bitten by a scorpion in Egypt in 1955." He proudly announced.

CHAPTER 9

This way to the Beach
Thailand

I couldn't write this book without my opinion and general analysis of Thailand, a country I lived and worked in for nearly 12 years, and a place I have frequently visited for over 30 years.

Travel is very subjective. What one person loves, another loathes.

But, having sampled numerous countries, I would say if you want the exotic, i.e., a tropical kingdom laced with gorgeous beaches, flavoursome cuisine, captivating culture and magnificent temples, not forgetting a pulsating nightlife, oh, and several bunk-ups. I would say visit Skyland.

I first touched down in 1982 and what a contrasting place it is now. Unfortunately for me, modern technology means even the poorest of the population now has 58-inch TV under their corrugated roof and a smartphone in their begging bowl with access to social media.

I don't mean that I begrudge them some creature comforts, but the country has lost its innocence for me. Maybe I'm a touch credulous to believe everything was rosy before, but their innocence is what I used to love about the place. The result of modern technology inevitably means that the materialistic world has arrived, and replaced the old life of Jack and the Beanstalk. For half of the people now, going to market to sell your cow or buy some, as (cow means rice in Thai) has now been replaced with going to market to trade-in your Merc.

The absence of a welfare state combined with general greed has produced the usual outcome; the rich get richer, and the poor get poorer. Resulting in both parties turning to unscrupulous means to fund their consumer lifestyle. Wealth maintenance methods available include business corruption, exploitation, violence, vice or politics. Sound familiar?

If you don't mind, I'll just put my cynicism on pause for a moment.

For me now, Thailand has become a paradox. As I said, the loss of innocence and some of its charm has, in my eyes, made Thailand somewhat stagnant for a repeat visitor like me. It's a bit like a great comedy being constantly aired on Dave. In the end, it becomes monotonous. Having said that, It's also like seeing your favourite old band; you want the all old songs, as the new stuff almost always disappoints.

That is why in this chapter you will find many contradictions because, when talking about Thailand, I become Siamese and wear two trilbys. You see, I have a love hat relationship with the place. But it's a country I keep going back to, so it must have some virtues. And for a first-time visitor, I still say it's up there with the best competition on the planet.

Shyland

After moving to Bangkok in 2001 and before I met my wife four years later, I have to admit to a semi-hedonistic lifestyle. As soon as I stepped off the plane, I entered the Rider Cup with Tiger, but regrettably he got caught. In my early years of being Thailish, I became vigorous and virile instead of the usual viral. The reason for this probably was the fact that back in the UK my lava flow had all but dried up and become dormant. So I decided to move to Thailand for some seismic action, where it became Krakatoa and Crackerjack every night.

I think being rather shy and reserved with the ladies back home had become a real psychological problem for me. You see, I was always the life and soul with the lads, usually making a right cunt of myself as the entertainment officer, but I never really knew how to talk to girls.

One of my problems was I always wanted Miss World, not Sharon from the Hoover factory, and although I would class myself a moderate catch, I suppose I was punching above my weight.

I reckoned to succeed with A-listers, you needed deep

pockets full of money, self-assurance and the keys to a car Clarkson's supplier would appreciate. Well, I had a couple of quid, a butchers bike and a pack of Polo, and way lacked self-confidence.

I would get into a sweat, even if a female smiled at me on the bus. Sure for men didn't work, and anyway it was uncomfortable wearing a leaf on your back. I wanted to be the Brad Pitt of the day. Not armpit.

It's so not fair nowadays; girls are much more forward since they stopped dancing around their handbags. Growing up at junior school, I still quite liked the Idea of notes under the table.

"If you love me, sign here" notes often made their way under the tables in our class, and unless it ended up in the teachers grasp, it was normally opened in the library. Because it was easier to face rejection with God's help under the R.E. section or be triumphal, even if I did get the obligatory "Shhhh boy."

Notes were a primitive version of Facebook if you like, and also a piece of piss to delete. To be jilted face to face at eleven was apocalyptic.

I think it all changed with girls' attitudes back in the nineties when Ibiza was uncovered. A whole new generation of ladettes were unleashed on the hordes of fat boy slims, sadly Just a couple of years too late for me. Having said that I think I would have had serious trouble swallowing smarties and drinking Evian with the Groove Rider just to get a shag. You can keep your dance, trance, jingle, jungle shite, but you can give me your house, garage, and greenhouse and sister's phone number.

Look, what's wrong with a fucking guitar!

At the disco in my day, when Don Johnson was still in pastels and JR was waiting for a bullet, it was normal to hunt for women by consuming a skin full of Courage, or Heineken (Dutch courage). Then take a taxi with your mates to the local night club, only to be, in my case, tortured by the shite music. So I would stand at the bar and consume ten more pints of piss while waiting patiently for the Keegan permed, horse teethed DJ to stick on the slow stuff. That would signal the pursuit of my prize, a stumble around with Lionel rich tea and Denise from Dunstable. You're once, twice, three times rejected!

If I was lucky, I might get her parents' phone number.

Forward to the following Wednesday

"Hello, Dunstable 533897."

"Hello it's Simon, can I speak to Denise, please?" Pause. . .

"No sorry, she's washing her hair, all year, goodbye."

I must admit I didn't help myself by acting the twat, which was a mask for rejection I suppose, and it always failed to impress the ladies. I think I was slightly misunderstood, ahead of my time! I was a mixture of Rick with the essence of Vivian on Neil's bike, in fact, I'll take the credit for the invention of alternative comedy. What do you mean put away your self-pity pills?

Back on the pull, it's not if I didn't get the look, I did, many times. I would blow a fortune on top clobber, and although a part-time slave to fashion, which went against my plastic punk principles, I liked to put my own signature on my look. Fashion turn to the left, fashion turn to the right. I was in the goon squad. Talking about songs I remember a line from a George Michael song for some reason that stuck with me 'sometimes the clothes do not make the man'. Shakespeare did the original 12" version sometime in the 1600s, but George could sing better and had his own brand in Asda.

Maybe in retrospect I was always trying too hard to look cool, giving off to what I perceived was an alluring, magnetic persona, the truth was I was filled with hidden timidity. I smoked Gitanes because Bowie did. With eighteen shoulder pads, I though I was major Tom. Turns out most of the girls I knew in later years commented, I looked more like Lee Evans in Linda Evans' jacket.

The upside to being single was, at least I wasn't like some of my mates. Already under the thumb at twenty-three. Plus, I was fucked if I was going to be attached to someone who's idea of a good time was visiting IKEA. Why would I want to go shopping for a new table with matching coasters for endless dinner parties? Sit round people's houses filled with a fashionable wine they couldn't pronounce, Oh, and the soundtrack to Dirty fucking Dancing. The pretentious evening culminating in a trivial board game in pursuit of a wedge. When alternatively I could be watching the mighty Hatters, or sitting watching Electric Blue with a beer in hand and knob in the other.

So when I arrived in Asia, it gave my right hand a well-earned rest. I was overcome with how easy it was to interact with females. Girls flung themselves at you in the bars, and I admit to lapping up all the attention. OK, I'm not stupid, although some may debate that, they had an agenda, but I was wise to it.

On most occasions, they never got their hands on my crown jewels. Because, although I was quite happy to share a bottle of beer, a laugh, and occasional bowl of grass, three letters were always in the back of my mind. HIV was, and still is, prevalent in S.E. Asia.

So I'd piss off to chat up women in nightclubs who worked in restaurants or shopping centres, as they were far more demure which gave me the upper hand. They were also normally from a reasonably educated background and keen to practice English and shagging.

OK, this plan was far from foolproof, and bottles of Singha don't offer as much protection as a strawberry ribbed tickler, that is in the judgment sense, not on the end of my helmet.

Slyland

Back in the days of indestructible youth I often felt the need to endanger myself every so often. For me the draw of Thailand and surrounding kingdoms twenty-five years ago were an intoxicating invitation. A gateway to the promise of wild adventures.

Although I once nearly got sent to jail without passing go. I used my chance card and flagged down a taxi driver outside the airport. My plan to save money with an unlicensed cab almost became a fatal mistake. We were stopped fifty clicks down the road by the police who subsequently discovered, in the lining of the doors, a years supply of Yaba, a class A methamphetamine worth about 100 big ones. Luckily the driver, after being hung, drawn and quartered, confessed under his last breath to being Muffin the mule. The confession left me extremely relieved to walk the 10k back to my hotel, only stopping to throw up and throw away my underpants.

Thailand has several mousetraps waiting for the inexperienced traveller, and, like any country that's not supported by welfare benefits, it's often embroiled with corruption. The survival of the fittest, dog eats dog (literally) with the emphasis placed on Wonga. Chances are you will get ripped off if you're not careful, but that's the general rule anywhere nowadays.

Occasional distressing incidents bring out the headlines in the red tops and as everywhere now, it's not immune to terrorism. But I would generally say it's still a very safe country to visit if you don't count the electricity network, no particular road rules and the fact that people who really don't need another drink will be served until their money runs out.

Thais are party people, and as the old saying goes, if you treat people as you would like to be treated yourself then you will find them more than accommodating.

Of course, the political troubles that rear up frequently of late are to be steered clear of, especially as it has fuck-all to do with us. But, as tourists you will certainly have a great time and go back hopefully with enduring memories. Weather wise, the sky can be indifferent, and the humidity is relentless, but when the sun has got its hat on it is as hot as their chillies. You will find most of the hotels are of superior quality in price compared to Europe, but service sometimes lacks.

The wonderful food is an explosion of colour and fragrance but laced with napalm so be forewarned, only ask for old spice after a shave. Unfortunately, public buses are driven by Brian from the Magic Roundabout, but the BTS train in Bangkok is decent, and taxis are cheaper than walking. Trips and tourist excursions cater for all budgets and general interests. Some of the attractions and treks are seriously worth a look.

Thailand is still a relatively cheap destination despite currency fluctuation. You can still do a holiday on a piggy bank full of sixpences, but don't forget your plastic). ATMs are more common than noodle stalls and credit cards are excepted everywhere even by some street vendors. Again, though use your acuity and be careful.

I once had a call from Nationwide Visa to say my card had been used to buy a ten grand wooden boathouse at a B&Q in Seoul. Last I heard, Korean police were looking for Justin Timberlake.

Expating in Thailand though is a different kettle of fish sauce. Doing business can carry a health warning. You have to screw your loaf as you are operating in an adult Disney world. Thailand attracts the usual suspects, nonces, gangsters and wannabe gangsters from around the globe, as well as the homegrown ones. Too many expats don't research enough and buy into a dream that turns into a nightmare. In general, if S.E. Asia is the mother of all consextionary shops, then Thailand is Willy Wanker.

The sex tourism industry goes back six centuries; history often quotes that prostitution is the world's oldest trade, funny I always thought boat building was! As I don't remember two whores walking Noah's gangplank. The bar scene properly kicked in and boomed during the Vietnam war, as Bangkok was used for major R&R.

Then other joints sprang up such as Pattaya and Phuket, later to be joined by a whole host of other whorehouses around the Pacific rim. One being the Philippines, which was used, and some say abused by uncle sam's boys at Clark air base.

Back in old Siam all tastes are on the menu, for in fact the sex trade probably accounts for 40% of all tourism in Thailand. Although the frequently changing powers that be wouldn't like to admit it. Asia may be known as the champion of the rag trade, but even they can't make enough dirty raincoats

Much has been written and documented about sex tourism in Thailand and most of it garbage, I might add. Especially from the sympathetic overtones of most authors or documentary makers regarding the poor old bar girl having to turn to tricks just to feed her offspring. More like feed her bank account. Unfortunately or, fortunately, depending on your holiday itinerary, the easy option is often taken by village girls to tie their buffalo up and hop on the bus and work the bars and massage parlours. This influx of diminutive labour is fuelled by Jackanory stories that prince charming will sweep them off their backs and provide for them and their family. I don't doubt this, and yes it does happen, but in the majority of liaisons, they won't meet Adam Ant, just tourists adamant on emptying their bollocks.

But, I'm not here to judge the morals and exploitation of, and by working girls. But I have to say I am still, dumbfounded by the legion of fuckwit expats who sign over a blank cheque and shower girls with bunches of karats. Fools gold would be more apt to describe these delusional midlifers in crisis. I mean mate, do yourself a favour and stop looking in the fairground mirror and get a real one.

What would a twenty year old cracker see in some middle to late aged, fat vest wearing, viagra popping loser? Wise up! If you're looking for sex fair enough, but if you're looking for love get yourself a David Niven accent and go cruise with Saga.

Despite my best efforts as a matrimonial and financial consultant, I failed to persuade many first timers of the pitfalls of the sweet shop. Maybe this is due to the fact I have a pretty negative attitude towards this subject, because I have seen shed loads of men put their misplaced trust, and trust funds, in the hands of a Barbie doll, only later to be left baht-less on the streets. As the British consul guy frequently liked to remind me over his cod and chips. "We are not a charity offering free repatriation for old dogs with two cocks!"

To live in Thailand, you have to know how to play the game.

I'm not saying all the girls or boys are bad, but as long as you understand it's a fair monetary exchange, i.e., cash for gash, and remember to keep your ATM under your false teeth mug, you'll have a good time. Also, there are thousands of young ladies working in shops and restaurants, as Mick Jagger said "That are just dying to meet ya."

If you're a tourist, especially a first offender, you may well meet what you think is your dream girl and soulmate. But remember as you gaze starry-eyed at your beloved on your iPhone on the flight home, she's probably on her back already. Once you arrive back home, please don't send her money. Even if her Buffalo's sick, her village has burned down, or she just wants a shiny new necklace. You see the reality is you are probably number five on her extortion list, after Gary from Gullibleshire.

How do I know? Well, my wife begrudgingly translated hundreds of these emails when we had our internet shop. However, if you accept that its all a bit of fun, and you won't be applying for a visa to take her round your mum's to meet Mr Kipling, then go for it.

If your taste is Boyzone, then the same rules more or less apply, but if your taste is for half man half biscuit, then great care must be taken. Yeah, some ladyboys look stunning but remember they carry more hormones than an oestrogen salesman and don't stumble back to their hotel drunk or drugged, as they often stay in the Fred West Wing.

One final gripe on this subject is for the endless expat balloon chasers scrounging their way around the birthday bar circuit for a free drink, or a leech at a sugar bush. Listen, mate just because you've spunked all your dosh from the sale of your council house on mongering and more wives than Henry the eighth, doesn't mean us, the restaurateurs, owe you freebies because of your misplaced assumption that we are the fucking salvation army.

There's a popular saying in Thailand, about taking a girl out of a bar for a new life back home in the UK. But nowadays I think it applies more to Westerners. "You can take the farang out of the bar, but you can't take the bar out of the farang."

So stop wearing your 'no money no honey t-shirt', and fuck off home to earn a living.

Going back to bar girls, the thing that most farang like is 90% of them offer the girlfriend experience without the baggage of a courting ritual, that is why the bars are so rammed in Slyland. Of course, they realise it's prostitution but It's not a cold transaction for sex like in most other cities. For most guys on a holiday like to hire one out, just like you do with a sunbed. They'll need to pay a bar fine and then they can take it home and lay on it.

But as I touched on earlier, beware the scammers who have perfected the art of seducing your ICA account then chewing you up and spending your will. Darling, I need some new clothes, darling I need more gold, darling my grandma's iron lung has rusted I need 20k for an operation and some emery cloth and so on. DON'T fall in love.

Listen, there are many expats who are happily married still living in Slyland, but there are also ten times more who have been fleeced. Remember when you play the game, you're on their turf. I don't mean to sound patronising, but you would be surprised how a pretty face turns the rational man irrational. So if that's your thang, play the game, don't be played.

A lot of the girls also have kids, or Thai boyfriends and husbands to feed. So it's customary for the children to be shipped up to the grandmas in Esaan as the income they receive from the escort industry is a fast track to land, house, and all the Uncle Bens they can eat.

Around my mid-twenties and when I'd moved on from counting my IQ on my fingers, I realised it didn't fucking matter what a person's sexuality was. Although I always play with a pretty straight bat, I have long held the opinion each to their own as long as it is within reason. And believe me, I have seen things that would make Paris Hilton blush. I could probably fill Wicks with shed loads of stories and experiences regarding Thailand. My mind seems to contain an a-z reference library of almost total recall. For example, pick a letter, any letter.

Although on second thoughts X may be a problem, don't know many stories involving a mother and daughter and a xylophone.

There were, however, some very real James Bond encounters with serious villains, including sipping cocktails with prominent former members of the six counties dispute. Men of equal reputation from the middle east. I also met some really interesting people with human stories, like North Korea's Steve McQueen, who gave me a lift on his motorbike.

Another drunken night of arm wrestling and three card brag with major Serg of Spetsnaz (Russian special forces).

"Simon, it took us ten fucking years to get out Afganistan, your war on terror is a recipe for a disaster," he said back in 2007. Um, he may have a point.

Luckily I had drunk up before Russian roulette began. I also stumbled into some of her Majesty's government, i.e., your representatives in various uncompromising positions, as well as plenty of celebs on the pull. Regrettably, all these files are stamped with top secret, as some of these tales, even now, could still lead me to a sleepless night with an equine head on my pillow. So I'll pass, that is until the Sun offers me 500k, a Guy Fawkes mask and a hack-less phone.

Songkran

Probably the biggest of tourist pulls for Thailand, besides little brown fuck machines is the Festival of Songkran, aka the Thai new year.

It falls around April the 13th. The date derives back to Tamil times, around 1000AD, when one of their top boys decided to invade parts of S.E. Asia. Etcetera, etcetera, etcetera! When his army had finished raping and pillaging and decided to catch the tide home, they left behind two useful pieces of Indian Civilization, a recipe for coconut curry and something called a calendar. This wasn't no Pirelli special with chariots of topless Bollywood beauties. No, this one was basically modeled on the cow jumping over the moon, and other celestial bodies. A lot later when Rama V1 (king of the day) came to power, he decided that the Thais should change the aforementioned calendar by restarting it from the moment Buddha expired.

It is loosely documented in the Tipitaka, that in 1471 Buddha had a rank mushroom bhaji. Apparently he went upstairs for a number 2 and never came down. Which all means that as I write this chapter in 2015, and if my maths are correct, which would be a first, 544 past years added to 2015 equates to the Thai year of 2559.

However, just to confuse you, the Thais also use the Christian calendar. Because, in 1941, the then PM decided to celebrate the Christian new year of January the 1st as well. Possibly so his wife could enjoy the sales. Got all that? Good.

Songkran is the cue for the party people of the world to descend on sunny Siam for festival frolics. It is also the cue for many expats to give a holiday to their libido, by flying home to escape a drenching. Oh and to gratify their cravings for great British institutions like Donner kebabs, Coronation Street and Sun Bingo. Not forgetting the most important aspect of their trip, a fabrication of their pension credits.

Chang Mai, the largest City in the north of Thailand, regularly hosts the most spectacular and ostentatious of all the celebrations with a lavish procession, accompanied by a week on the lash, this is not to be confused with getting lashed in Malaysia, a much more painful experience. The festival is replicated to a slightly lesser extent in most cities and towns around the kingdom.

The most famous aspect of the Songkran celebrations is the throwing of water. The custom originates from spring cleaning aspect of Songkran. Part of the ritual was the cleaning of images of Buddha. Using the 'blessed' water to sprinkle lightly on other people, it was seen as a way of paying respect and bringing good fortune. Nowadays it's turned into hydro wars, with the tourists toting huge plastic water canons. The battles normally rage on for three to seven days.

A very small minority of Thais like to use Songkran as a whiskey drinking competition that often turns them into Gene Hackman, as they go on a machete murder-fest, normally (thank goodness) amongst themselves.

A large number of deaths are also common on the roads, with the annual Sang Som (Rum) TT race, when hordes of paralytic kamikaze moped drivers lose their marbles and their lives. But in general despite these small misdemeanors, in the main it's a joyous occasion, and the vast, vast, majority have a great fun.

Then as the clock strikes 6 pm each evening the Geneva convention is stringently adhered to, and there is a cease-fire to hostilities.

All foes down weapons and meet in the road to exchange condoms, and play football, and then it's a quick mop and sponge up, and the bars become rammed again. It always struck me as strange that a country that suffers from huge water shortages, despite heavy monsoon months, likes to recreate Venice without pigeons by wasting such an important commodity like H_2O. Hopefully, many of you reading this chapter may well have sampled Songkran; I have already touched on the meaning and madness of the event, but for those of you who haven't, and to give you an understanding of mayhem to these festivities. I first need to go back to 1996.

I merrily bowled down Soi 4, Sukhumvit Road, Bangkok. It was a hot April morning; I was heading to pick up a copy of the local rag when I was the victim of a horrendous attack.

From out of nowhere a stealth pickup truck containing the Thai 'A Team' launched an all out aqua attack with multi-bucket launchers, pump action water hoses, and automatic water pistols. In fact, any water vessels bigger than an egg cup. Mr T, doubling as the phantom flour flinger, then rained tiger balm cluster meringues down on me just to finish the job. I lay defenceless, floundering on the ground; I looked up to a group of tourists with seal pup eyes, fuck I hope they're not Canadians I thought.

Fast forward to April 2004, I had been living in Bangkok now for a couple of years and had become a Songkran veteran. However, this year was to be extra eventful, for not only was Bangkok getting wet, but it was also getting my mother and father on their first visit to the Kingdom.

09:32 Tuesday, April 14. I awoke with a Tasmanian devil of a hangover that he'd given to me for my over-indulgence with my other drinking mate James Boag. Mr Boag is not a person known to me, but a Hobart brewed pilsner I surprisingly found hidden last night in the Pink Pussy Bar's antique fridge.

I could see the sky was awake, and the currant bun was

burning a hole in my seahorse embroidered nets. I turned over the other way to block out the sun's glare; my eyes refocused on my bedroom door, it had a blue dress hanging on it?

Strange! Then another thought flickered inside my pounding head, where the fuck am I? The lyrics to Talking Heads' Once in a Lifetime sprang to mind. This is not my beautiful house; This is not my beautiful wife. Oh yeah, I'm in the Dynasty Grand Hotel Bangkok.

I struggled, rocking to get up, and as I sat on the edge of my mattress, I turned to survey the wreckage of my trashed room. A new question arose. Had I partied with the Beastie Boys last night? There were items of clothing strewn across the floor, and the furniture looked like it had a punch up with a poltergeist. On the table lay a huge red and yellow plastic rocket launcher, a handbag, a half eaten fish, plus a snazzy looking SLR camera. I stood up which then extended into a full on yawn. Luckily I hadn't thrown the TV in the swimming pool but it looked like I had brought up the deep end up last night. I stretched across my bed for my underpants.

Wait a minute, who's been sleeping in my bed? Not fucking Goldilocks that's for sure. A long black hair occupied one of my pillows and a there was also a small indent in the mattress. Then the sound of the toilet flush startled me. Now let me think, what happened last night? I partly remember stumbling out of Lucifer's Bar to visit the Cockwell Inn, but after that, it was blank.

The Lock unclicked and from my bathroom emerged my new companion who waded back to the bed wrapped in a bedsheet, she smiled and collapsed face down on the mattress. A large shaft of sunlight powered up my room, and I could see her cute little brown arse was winking at me. She turned on her side and with inviting hamburger. Must be time for breakfast.

I climbed on, and after my brief tongue hanging out Alsatian impression, collapsed in exhaustion. Face to face, she opened one eye.

"You finish yet?"

I nodded, panting.

"Morning, er" I said trying to remember her name. She continued

"Why you no remember me, Adolf?"

"Of course, I remember you, darling," I said, playing for more time, and who the fuck's Adolf, I thought.

Suddenly my recollecting was interrupted by a loud knock on the door.

"Simon, are you coming down for breakfast" enquired mum.

Shit, I'd forgot about mum and dad being in the next room. In hindsight not the best move by me. I had just got rid of my great Aunty Cath and her fifty plus daughter, Matilda, who had to come and spend a few days with me from a sheep station near Canberra. Apparently they have been to Samui in the eighties. I tried to hint diplomatically to mum that Soi 4, Nana Plaza Bangkok was not an idyllic place. In fact, it was a place for the vice squad, rather than a place for the 2nd coming of bible bashing Aussies, but it fell on deaf ears.

I had discussed my displeasure the previous evening at dinner with my parents and why they had sentenced me to chaperone the Amish around Bangkok. At least my mum and dad open to most things and liberal minded although I think mum was getting a bit fed up with the attention dad was getting from girls he would have once built a dolls house for.

Mum knocked again. Right, Don't panic Mr Mannering I said to myself.

"Er yeah, be there in ten to fifteen minutes mum, gonna jump in the shower first". I called back.

"Simon can you please open the door love, I need your dad's camera," insisted mum.

"Er, sorry mum, no can do. I'm in the nude". I flimsily replied.

"Don't worry love, I'm sure it nothing I haven't seen before."

"Wanna fucking bet", I thought!

I sat in the bathtub under the intermittent shower of drip, drip, squirt, blast, cold, warm, fucking scalding. I sighed, F.F.S, I didn't have the energy or patience to try and regulate the flow of my Meccano apparatus. Why is it hotels always fit their fucking bathrooms with the most ridiculous of taps? On/off that's all we need, not a fucking espresso machine. I sat on the toilet; the Japanese POW torture kit had helped to bring back my memory; The girl's name was Yong Lee, a Thai-Chinese bird from the Witches Tit, the last bar I had visited around five am I reckon. I sat motionlessly; another thought rushed in, fuck, I hope I haven't taken any readers wives pictures on dad's Nikon.

The door then knocked again, loudly. This time it was Dad

"Simon, I need my camera, can you pass it to me."

I looked up from my crouching tiger position to see a brown body sporting a tea towel shuffling past my bathroom entrance towards the door.

'DON'T OPEN THE FUCKING DOOR."

I apologised to Yong Lee and swallowed a concoction of pineapple and paracetamol and accompanied this with several belches and Brahms 5th bottom concerto.

"You vely bad German manner fat dog man," said Yong Lee in a fairish comment.

But German? Vorsprung Durch Sexknic! I then presumed that it was in reference to my Alsatian rut?

No surely not, I re-evaluated, she would have no comprehension of Alsace, maybe she's fucked a real German shepherd.

After a ten minute discussion, I managed to persuade her to "Get in ze shower." I quickly invented some pathetic excuse about a man and shepherd's pie, then forced her into a quick change. I made a swift business transaction, adding a little extra for my scratch and sniff concert and then led her downstairs to the entrance of the lobby. Then not wanting to be spotted by my parents with Yong Lee hooker, I doubled back and jumped over the wall and re-entered the Hotel by the kitchen.

10:56.

"Sleep well?" I enquired.

"Yes, thanks, like a log," said dad, giving me a knowing look as if he knew what I'd been up.

I revisited my Kama Sutra memories.

I was brought back to the present and my hangover at the table when mum enquired, "any more tea dear?"

"No thanks, pass the coffee please, my head feels like the elastic in a golf ball."

But she was multi-tasking; reading a book, nibbling toast and telling flies off.

"Ah that's nice dear." She said. Then suddenly stood up.

"Right Joe, come on, its time for shopping."

Dad looked a taken back a bit and said. "What, my bun?"

I had booked them on several trips and today was market day. I warned them the traffic would be extremely heavy, and they would probably get wet today as Songkran was still winding down.

"It was yesterday; it was like a biblical scene Simon, the road to Damascus." Laughed mum.

"Well, today make sure you take your rain macs, as it could be the parting of the seas."

After a couple of minutes rubbing my thumping Gallway, I stood up. It was stifling and 39 degrees already. I decided to head straight for the pool. The flimsy steps swayed as I gingerly descended, and then I slipped and turned my leap into an Orca the Whale Impression. The row of occupied sunbeds directly behind my entrance were not amused.

I wallowed around for a bit then abruptly stood up, oh shit my breakfast was regurgitating, I think I'm going to be sick. Lucky the pool was empty, except for me and my Heinz big soup I had just emptied from my mouth. I frantically scooped out the larger bits with my cupped hands and flung it under a potted palm at the water's edge. Within seconds Indian Myna birds were feasting, it made me feel better to help starving animals.

I lay on a sun bed recuperating, out of sight from the pool by a small lake when a rogue ladyboy abruptly ambushed me.

"Hello, sexy man my name is. . ."

Before she could finish her sentence I made my excuse and broke Johnathan Edward's world record to get the toilet. I promised myself religiously while hiding on the shitter that I would never drink to excess again! Who was I kidding?

But it did beg the question, why do we always spunk so much money on booze, knowing full well the next day will have debilitating consequences? For me, there are very few reactions that replicate the feeling of near death so well as a super hangover.

14.17

Bangkok, oriental setting and the city don't know what the city is getting, played Murray Head from the old radio behind the bar. Feeling out of ICU now after consuming a hairy dogs cocktail. I'm anchored to the pool bar. The speaker continued to crackle.

One night in Bangkok and the tough guys tumble.

Can't be too careful with your company.

I can feel the Devil walking next to me.

Too true, the monster from the black lagoon was back. Time to get my spikes on again.

14.46

My parents returned.

"How was your shopping trip?" I enquired.

"It was all tat, so we didn't bother much, we just went for a long walk," said dad. "But I did buy a copy Rolex for John next door, do you think he'll like it?"

"Yeah, nice," I said, but pondered if it was allowed. I'm sure it says in the New Testament that thy shall not bear false watches against thy neighbours."

15:42

"Where you come from?" Said the masseur.

"Sweden," I replied.

"You want oil massage?"

"Yeah, yes please."

"How much you give me? 800 baht OK."

"No way "50 crowns," I said.

"You want a happy ending?"

"Oh definitely."

"Then it's 800 baht Mr, no clowns!"

"OK nice one" I laughed, she was right by being wrong.

The masseur's name was Goung (Prawn); she was about twenty-two and fit; she had two great claws. She started to pummel and pull me around and then slowed to pander my meat and veg with sensual oils under the umbrella in the shade of the bamboo hut and the coconut tree.

"Simon I got you an ice cream?"

"NOT NOW MUM."

In a flash, I flipped onto my front and grabbed the cornetto like a crocodile taking a wildebeest from a river.

"I'm having a massage mum."

"Yes, I can see that dear, but I just wanted to tell you that some girl was trying to get into your room, but I told her that the room was Simon's, not Adolfs."

CHAPTER 10

Food for thought

Thinking to myself "Having dined around the world from the humble street stall to Michelin gaffs, what would you say is the best food or meal you've ever eaten and where?" Googling my head for an internet connection, I answered. "Tell you what, probably a more interesting question would be what's the strangest food you've ever eaten, as a good meal is often a reflection of one's mood, location and company."

As generally a greedy bastard, I've always been in love with food and if I had to choose between sex, drugs and Roquefort roll. The last one gets my vote, as long as the roll is Brioche. There is a common belief you can beat an egg, but you can't beat a wank. This statement does have some validity but have you tried Cadburys?

Food Glorious food. Firstly I have to say I have been lucky and grown up with a healthy selection box of interesting grub.

Mum and dad didn't drink, gamble or have many vices, so they blew their spare dosh in Marks and Spencer, who even back in the seventies filled their shelves with some top Tucker. Add to this my uncles were serious wine heads, which all meant we ate handsomely at home and on family visits to the relo's estate. At the tender age of 13 I was introduced to Bollinger, Chablis and Fleurie while everybody else in my social circle was swigging Old English, Black Tower and Lambrusco. I hope that statement doesn't sound like grandiloquence, as nothing could be further from the truth.

My parents lived in a modest house on a modest wage but when it came to food they had excellent taste. A perk of having rich relatives back in the seventies was that Boxing day round my uncles meant a full Harrods spread with bottles of grape water worth more than dad's car. All washed down with snooker, Hennessey XO and Havana's.

I never felt it spelled the death of alphabet spaghetti; it just gave me the opportunity to appreciate some of the finer things in life.

When I eventually flew the nest and got my own pad, one of the joys of being independent, was that I loved experimenting in the kitchen. This meant I would often invite the gang round for a slap up nosebag or a BBQ.

In later years when Jamie came on the scene and wowed

THE SEARCH FOR THE GOOSE'S PALM

the youth of the day with Indie cooking, I thought, I wish I'd done that ten years ago. I don't mean a TV a chef, although I can cook. I meant educating my peers to the joys of real food, and although I'd have preferred a Harley to a Vespa, we were singing from the same cookbook. In my early youth, most of the time I kept my knowledge quiet as there was is a lot of snobbery around food and wine especially back in the day. As I mentioned, I came from your average working class background, as did most of my friends and their families. Regarding the lads, for them a trip to Wimpey or the local cafe was dining out!

Kebabs and curry nights became popular, but a visit to places like an Aberdeen Steakhouse was the absolute dogs.

I always remember, once in Aberdeen's Oxford Street branch when I was about seventeen, I chose Tornado Rossini from the menu while the lads were considering some crap like Spam Supreme or the usual suspects. I persuaded them to try Chicken Kiev, they were 10 minutes hesitant but eventually agreed. I placed my order with an Italian waiter, at first the lads thought I'd made a joke to him about a football player in the ongoing '78 world cup.

So when my dish arrived, I got comments like, "Urgh, are you gay?" Or something along the lines of, "You wouldn't catch me eating that foreign shit, it's full of that garlic stuff."

"Yeah you're probably right boys, just stick with your Chicken Kevin."

We all know generally Britain in the seventies had crap food, with uninspiring recipes and fishy cooking programs like Cradock's Fanny. I'm trying not to be condescending but for a lot of people a Spagbol was an Italian, a Chinese was a number 42 and a Vesta an Indian. Then cooking with Kerr hit our screens 'The Galloping Gourmet', a sort of imported forerunner for Floyd and others, with plenty of slurping.

I even bunked off school to watch him until Betamax came knocking. The TV screens then exploded over the next fifteen years with cooking the filling for daytime TV, Red pepper, green pepper, red lorry, yellow lorry, In the end it spread like a giant Yorkshire onto to prime time.

I remember Brain Sewell on Masterchef describing a contestant's dish as gross man, funny I thought that was the presenter. Let's see who lives in a fucking big house like this? Celebrity chefs that's who! They are now on a par with overpaid, exposed footballers, competing every year for the Poêle d'Or (golden frying pan). Hang on this could get Messi.

In literature, back in the day Mrs Beaton's cookbook was the known as the original Bible, I remember we had one holding up the broken foot on mum's bed. Beaton was in every household, but she was hardly a goddess. She may have had bigger books than Nigella, but I doubt if anyone ever had a tug over her muffins.

For me, travel and food go hand in hand. My general education from encountering contrasting cultures is also generally entwined around the diversity of their gastronomic offerings

Reflecting on my culinary voyage across the seven seas, I'd have to say some pretty strange things have entered my mouth.

Frankie says. . . "Ooh er Mrs, now then, No, no, listen, behave. Oh, please yourselves."

I was noshing on shite long before celebrities in the Jungle, and even now when I visit the zoo, I often feel quite guilty. One of my favourites is the Indonesian toffee apple (rat on a stick).

I also highly recommend Philippino Balut, live duck embryos boiled in their shell, but not Tiger's cock, (stick to Frosties).

Although being up for most things, and having the constitution of Billy Bunter, there was no way I was having the hot dog in Seoul.

Most of the planets offal I have consumed has normally had its identity hidden from me by foreign language menus. But sometimes it's been eaten with alcohol fuelled, frontier style bravery. The quickest way to douse my reservations and my taste buds.

Nowadays we often see culinary fads and fashions come along, with swanky restaurants in say 5th Avenue, or Chelsea making reviews in Time Out for their flame grilled Baboon's flange.

It's normally overcooked and overpriced, and they almost always revert to œufs et des frites (egg 'n chips), remember, you can't beat an egg.

I think the general rule for food is that most of the stuff you find in Waitrose is there for a reason, it tastes nice! Meaning all the other crap I force fed myself was an experience but usually not a pleasure.

On the liquid front, I've also sampled a few strange cocktails and portions of soup in my time. There's a bit in the book The Beach, where the hero drinks snakes' blood in Bangkok. Well, I never came across it there, but I did in Southern China. Warm cobra's blood mixed with cheap whiskey and honey. Apparently it's supposed to give you the ultimate hard on, like a Viagra thick shake, but all it gave me was a hard day's night, with continual trips for a hiss. Then there was the 'Kermit Shandy' in Costa Rica, which was a mixture of local beer and poison from a tree frog. This carried a hallucinogen warning. Luckily I only had one glass and flew straight home on the back of a giant toucan.

If you like soup, I recommend the Dominican mountain chicken consume. Consisting of lizard, cane toad and coconut rum. "Bootiful". I had seconds, and seconds later produced the hugest fart I've ever heard. I measured 8.4 on the Ripper scale, and as it echoed through the mountains, the staff ran for the shelters thinking Monserrat had blown up again.

Fast food is not a favourite of mine. However, it does stir amusing memories of India. In Rajasthan, I had ordered two-quarter pounders in our hotel cafe, because the house special, which roughly translated to goldie aloo, meant that you would soon be looking for one.

Even though my McDelhi whoppers turned out to made from 100% wall paper paste, (cottage cheese). I settled for them, as that the rest of the group who scoffed Blue Peter's old dog ended up as I suspected, modeling Andrex for the next three days.

Then there was the time in New York. We had got lost on

the Subway looking for a recommended burger joint, so Les, our fearless mate from Rochdale, just bowled up to a street gang sat on the A train and asked for directions.

Their initial reaction changed from "Hey man, what's in your bag?' To "Hey man, it's Crocodile fucking Dundee." An easy mistake, as Rochdale is twinned with Ramsey Street. He ended up with a five points handshake plus a Mets cap.

The worse place I've ever been for food was Cuba. I had arranged an all-inclusive hotel for the chaps but forgot to take into account years of sanctions. You know there's something wrong when the KGB leftover from the cold war left the leftovers, even Oliver Twist stayed seated.

For dessert, there's only one place, and that's Amsterdam, their cakes are hand rolled from an old recipe handed down from NASA apparently. A must try, accompanied by a buzz light beer.

I must admit the subject of foody fun is up there with a triple half pike, in the degree of difficulty in deciding my favourite story. Let's think. Um, I think it would probably have be a fry up between Japanese sashimi, or Casablanca tea party.

Right, I just flipped my fortune cookie, and Tokyo Joe took the second biscuit.

Tokyo Joe

My friend Ben was visiting me in Bangkok. So during a heavily ale infested evening we decided, as you do, we would visit Japan tomorrow. The next morning we sloped off to the travel agents.

We ended up plumping for a ten-day tour. Three nights Tokyo, same again in Osaka, ending with a four-night stay in Kobe.

The flight was at 5 pm and pretty reasonable with United, but the hotels were expensive, as was the beer, well everything really. The language was a problem, as the Jap's grasp of English was surprisingly poor and my Japanese even poorer. This consisting of super-fly, Super-dry, and odd words I picked up in the hide and seek game Pikachu.

Ben and I arrived at Narita Airport and grabbed a taxi, as we couldn't understand the underground metro map, plus we didn't have any gas masks. I did try to learn some basic language, but Japan helpfully has three, however, hello goodbye, thank you, etc., were reasonably pronounceable.

The next morning on our first trip I met a tour guide from Hiroshima, who actually, spoke great English, probably because she was married to a Melburnian. I sat out one of the offloads to watch a Japanese wedding and chatted to her on the coach about the many ways of the rising sun.

She told me that not many people spoke English because being a financial exporting powerhouse they didn't see why they needed to bother. In fact she said, the last English spoken by anyone in her town dates back to the mayor, who in 1945 shouted "What the fuck was that?" In all seriousness, she just seemed to accept what had happened in the war from both sides and told me that the Japanese didn't hate the Americans, despite half of her family being nuked. "A dog doesn't hate its master." She quoted, but we still concurred economically. Still the Imperialist, I thought.

She carried on and told me since the financial crash hit in the nineties, and the recession had swept through business, opinions had now changed, and you couldn't swing a Shi-Tzu for English teachers.

On returning from the city tour, we rested then showered, changed and read the earthquake emergency procedures. This alerted us not to use the lifts or the stairs and not to panic. The best plan was to try and call International Rescue, but if Brains was engaged up Joe 90 again, you should tie your bedsheets together, and climb out of the window. What, on the 12th floor?

Our first stop that night was Electric town, a very long street where you can find all the latest gadgets including the latest NS 5 from I Robot.

After a noodle stop, we hit a bar that turned out to be owned, peculiarly we thought, by an Iranian. We noticed lots of English football memorabilia and several football scarves adorning the walls; Man Utd, Liverpool, Chelsea, and Walsall! The owner told us that many English fans had visited his bar during the 2002 world cup and left him various souvenirs. Regarding Walsall, he told us his best customers were Barry and Brian from Sutton Coldfield, and they had bestowed upon him the presidency of the unofficial Saddlers' supporter club of Asia.

A prestigious award indeed, I congratulated him.

Talk of the world cup reignited a discussion about David Beckham's toe injury and a multitude of other subjects including his homeland. He told us he had to do a runner from Tehran in '79, as the revolutionary guard had refused to pay their bar bill. He also stated proudly, that he missed the Shah and had a signed photo of him on the wall.

"Think I prefer the Walsall scarf," said Ben.

That comment signalled the bill, but I did give him my Luton Town pin badge. We headed to Roppongi, the Soho of Tokyo. The first place we entered was an exclusive club. I noticed when we signed the register it was scribbled with so-called dignitaries from around the world. Basically, it was a high-class knocking shop. I'm not sure why we didn't just go into a normal bar, but this place just looked interesting from the outside.

Once inside, it was set out super plush with international beauties spread around like in a Bond film. The drinks tariff was extortionate.

A flute of shampoo was around 50 quid, and if you wanted the company of a hostess, say Miss Saigon, the price was £200 for a thirty minutes chat. That's a 100 quid a word!

We shared a Seven-up, stirred not shaken, and left £20 lighter.

A lot of bars in Tokyo are entered from a ground floor lift that then climb two or three stories and open directly into the bar.

One such bar we entered was such and called Julius Berger. The prices were still high, but tolerable. The barmaid was named Tula, a lovely Dutch blonde who was very welcoming and engaging, but she soon attracted the wrath of the boss who I figured by his accent was probably African.

He was barking orders from behind the optics, and then he appeared and looked straight at me. How the hell did he get a visa? I thought. I know one shouldn't prejudge, but maybe he could read my mind, as he stared at me like I was a white farmer. That gave me the impression that he was straight from Mugabe's ANU hit squad.

I went for a Piss, and on my return noticed a photo of the same guy on some sort of license on the wall next to the bar. It was in Japanese obviously, but it had his mug shot with a red date stamped on it, which was up tomorrow as it happened. I strolled back and joined Ben. We couldn't help noticing the owner repeatedly scolded the girls for trivial things, and then he was embarrassingly rude to a customer.

Another barmaid, a Czech girl, called Monica started to well up when the customer flung his change at her. I'm not surprised the bar was 90% empty with this owner's customer relation skills.

After he'd fucked off, I enquired with the staff about the Rhodesian Ridgeback. The guys name was Joseph, and he was actually from Nigeria, but he had spent time in Zimbabwe and South Africa, accounting for his strange accent. His brother Michael was the owner; Joe was only the manager. I asked the girls a few other general questions regarding Tokyo nightlife and then inquired as to the name of the bar, Julius Berger? Monica said, apparently it was named after a football team in Lagos.

"No shit?" I said. "How is that going to fit into a chant?"

"Don't joke about it," she said. "These guys are fruitcakes, especially about football."

"Are they Walsall supporters?" Asked Ben.

"Shhh," hissed Tula.

"So why work here then?" Ben asked. "It's not easy to get a job cash in hand," answered Monica. Ben ordered our next beers and drinks for the girls.

Tokyo Joe (named by Ben) then came back into the bar and started again on Monica about collecting a lone glass. It was then I hatched an 'imperceptive plan', to darn well take him down a peg, or as we say nowadays, make him look a twat.

My thoughts on his character ranged from fucking ignorant prick to total cunt, so I decided to put him right.

I called him over. "Woz up man," I said in my best New York MTV hip-hop accent, and offered my hand in the shape of a fist.

I absurdly carried on. "Why chu acting so dead arse? Chill out. Bro, the chicks are cool." I persevered, but then lost my geography over the Bermuda triangle and turned up as Geoffrey Boycott in York. "Just relax Joe lad, and have brew wit me, leave lassy be."

I shut my eyes, shit, that was more Tetley tea than Ice-T.

He leaned on the bar with one elbow and stared directly into my face; Ben kicked my leg under the bar.

"Err, guess you the boss then?" I enquired, as myself.

He gave me the, what the fuck you are talking about, Willis?" expression. Then said "Yeah man, that's right bro, who wants to know?"

He stood back up; "No offence mate," I said cheerily. "Listen, your name is Joseph, right?"

"Yeah" he answered,"

"And you're from Lagos right?"

He nodded, then frowned and became circumspect. "How do you know dis, you the fucking FBI?"

I took an intake of breath, "Joseph, keep calm mate, I'm not a Yank, I'm English, and it's like this, you're wearing a football shirt with your name on the back!"

He thought for a while; then a huge smile broke over his face followed by some serious teeth sucking ending with a booming laugh.

I quickly whipped out my fake Scotland Yard/MI6 plastic card, which I had had made in Khaosan Road to entertain Thai bar, girls. In full flow now, I preceded to introduce us. "My my name is, my name is Detective Inspector Reagan, and this is Sergeant. . . the real Slim Shady" I said Eminem style. "Collectively known, as the Flying Squad."

Ben gave me a look of shock at my insane introduction. Joseph deciphered my rhythmical rigmarole for a while and then burst out laughing again. "Brother, if you's police, then I am Muhammed Ali, but you sure is one crazy joke man." He quipped.

Now you would think to be one nil up against Juliues Berger, I would have, and should have, parked my bus. But Instead I went on the offensive and ended up scoring an own goal.

"Now Listen, Joseph, If I might be serious," I said with straight a face . "Can you do me a favour mate and treat the girls with a bit more respect, OK," I said. "Or I won't be renewing your liquor licence."

"The fuck you talking otu?"

"The red one on the wall, it runs out today mate."

He thought for a nanosecond then exploded. "That's de fucking hygiene toilet licence man."

With that, I grabbed a returning Ben and although we weren't drinking Strongbow we made a sharp exit to the lift. Where's Kato when you need him! The doors shut in the nick of time. We travelled down and out onto the pavement, running straight for five minutes into the neon night.

We sat in a small street cafe with a coffee not speaking for three songs on the radio. "Sorry Ben, that was crazy. Come on, let's find somewhere else, I promise to be a good boy."

He reluctantly laughed and shook his head and said, "You'd better, Simon because that was off the fucking head."

I later found out 'Otu' means a front bottom in Nigerian, about right then!

Argy Bargy

Next stop for a Craic an Irish bar. A few pints of black stuff later we wandered into a small local bar run by Mr Shiitake San, a fungi from Nagoya. Well, that's what we called him. By now you will have guessed I like to give people nicknames, you've probably got one for me!

We were joined at our table by three señoritas from South America, who turned out to be privileged IT girls. One of them was the Argentinian Ambassador's daughter, and she was showing me a lot of attention. We chatted for a while. Her name was Claudia. I introduced Ben and She in turn her two friends, Lola and Marina.

She told me that her dad was loaded, I said "In that case. I'll have a rum and Coke."

She said "Fine" and in thirty seconds time she said, "I want to live like common people."

Naturally I told her my that name was Jarvis.

In reality, we small talked about South America and to show my knowledge off, I told her I always liked watching Boca Juniors; she told me she loved River Plate. For the non-football fans amongst you, it's nothing to do with Michael Flatley. These are the two main teams in Buenos Aires separated geograph-ically by the River Plate. It's rich vs poor, and they hate each other with a vengeance, it makes City v Utd look pedestrian.

Never mind, I thought. I never much liked West Side Story.

We ended up in a large whisky style karaoke bar they often frequented.

It was very similar to the one in the movie Black Rain but without Michael Douglas. It was oval in shape and had a huge glass bar stacked up with Scotch at one end. Around the walls were plenty of tables that circled the raised dance floor that supported a live band; again it was mega expensive. The three girls ordered a bottle of 12-year-old Dimple and a jug of Coke. That is the funny thing in the East, and even though they were South Americans, everybody in Asia loves their single malts or vintage dam drowned in coke or soda.

Rab C Nesbit would be crying in his pint of Thunderbird.

We looked at the drinks menu, shit, 90% in Nihongo, so I ordered a bottle of JD as I recognised the label, and we shared their Coke.

That was ninety quid! Time for my plastic friend again. Turned out their Dimple was £250, but daddy's million yen tab had their check covered. Then the last friend of Tom Cruise wondered over to our table. He was very tall for a Jap; he had long grey hair tied in a ponytail with a craggy face, and a menthol Mild Seven clamped between his assorted gold teeth. He bowed like a Samurai then smiled and stretched out his ruby-clad fingers and placed song request sheets on our table to be filled out.

We decided to call him, not surprisingly, Sam.

Ben San soon got up and did his obligatory Elvis song, but I hid in the Venus fly trap. Funny I've always had a fantasy of being a lead singer in a rock band and being worshipped by underwear throwing females. Unfortunately, my singing is so awful; I was forced to take up the comb and tissue, which never attracted birds only mating bees. Having said that, I did play the bass poorly in our Bay City Rollers tribute band back at school. . . and We sang Shang a Lang. After about two hours of listening to wock'n'woll singers, the alcohol was taking effect. This place was totally surreal, in fact, the whole evening was. The girls ordered another bottle of Dimple and a bottle of Veuve, God knows what their old man earned.

We entered into the high spirits phase of getting shitfaced and enthusiastically discussed Madonna's Evita, Che's T-shirts and Delmonte vs Fray Bentos, that's corned beef, not more football teams. Luckily, even pissed, I managed to steer well clear of the one subject guaranteed to bring Englishman and Argentinian alike to violent confrontation . . . Never once did I mention Maradona's deliberate handball. Then Sam came over with his hostess, Lauren, a French beauty in a sparkling shower curtain. She said there was a buffet and if we were hungry to help ourselves.

Ben went scouting and came back chicken nugget-less. "It's all alien to me," he said. "Lots of Sushi and strange looking creatures with rice and noodles. Do you reckon they got Walkers?"

Then Sam was back at the table again, "Why you not eat?" He said, in a rather skinny suit camp way.

"Err we're not hungry, thank you," I said, "We had lunch with Terry Aki earlier."

"OK, I get you a surprise," he said.

"At last, beans on toast!" Said Ben, only half joking.

"You vulgarian," I said, stretching the vocabulary a bit."

You are Bulgarian Ben?" Asked Lola, confused.

"No, it means Ben pretends to be well-bred, but he's a peasant really," I explained.

Sam returned with a small plate of bits of fish. "Try this, this make you big power tonight!" He said and winked.

"What is it?" I asked.

"This is very, very special fish, cost big dollar in your country, but I let you try free, OK." He slapped my back. "We call it sashimi," he continued, "very delicious, come from number one chef, Mr Agahsi."

"Wasn't he the bloke in Karate kid?" Said Ben, seriously.

I gingerly put a piece in my mouth. He then offered it to Ben who took two bits. It didn't have much flavour, just salty from the soy sauce, so I smiled, and half bowed but declined any more. Ben moved on to a bowl of noodles then the Argy girls explained to me that the sashimi dish I'd just tried was fugu, a very dangerous pufferfish that kills many people every year.

WHAT THE FUCK? I sprinted to the toilet and tried to make myself sick. I returned twenty minutes later feeling a little bit like I was at sea on a tyre in a force ten. Ben, by now polluted, was just grinning. "You gotta go sometime mate," he slurred.

I was in a panic; Claudia poured me two vessels of shampoo, and they never touched the sides, it acted as a tranquilliser, and after an hour had passed I felt in a better plaice, place.

The Argie girls and Claudia kept assuring me, "Simon, don't worry, they have a special chef with a license to prepare this fish, you'll be fine but don't try anymore!"

ANY MORE? "There is more chance of me getting up with the band and playing chopsticks on Sam's' teeth, or doing a duo with Carl Douglas."

Then, speak of the devil, Sam and Lauren hijacked me and forced me to sing. The band were unfamiliar with Geordie classics, so 'Who shall have a fishy on the little dishy' was shelved. I chose a rendition of killing me softly.

Too bloody true, I went for the Fugees, or should I say the Fugu's version, as it had more street cred, and I thought the locals would be down with Nip Hop. Fuck knows what the band were playing though as they had Animal from the Muppets on the drums.

I finished with a Yo Arigatou Mother Fucker, and bowed several times.

It received polite applause, as always in Japan, and I triumphantly returned to my seat. Churchill waving to my adorning Geisha groupies.

About 2 am, I was sufficiently slaughtered to enter the arena of the dance floor with Claudia. She had requested salsa music from the resident band, Haribo and the Sour Notes, who were accompanied by the house dancing girls, Panasonic people. Now salsa is not one of my favourites genres of music. When I was in Latino land, I was the only one still at the bar, as my mates, and the whole place went nuts going loco down to Acapulco.

I started with slick demented moves I pulled from a Wigan Pier youtube clip and threw in a few shapes. The heady atmosphere and the hypnotic beat of Dr Beat turned me into a wild and rugged Antonio Banderas character, so I re-enacted my infamous Tenerife show stopping Matador Trance dance.

Grabbing a table cloth and becoming the Bull, Toros, Toros, Toros. Strangely, just like back in 1984. Unfortunately, it had the same outcome.

After an Oscar-winning gyrating performance of the dying beast, I careered out of control and into the band, head butting the sax player. Last time it was the organ player.

Claudia was not impressed, in fact, she was the one seeing red! She lobbed a Goose Green grenade at me, (her stiletto). Silly cow I thought, oh no, that was me! She swiftly paid her bill, picked up her shoe and called me Inglés estúpido idiota torpe. (probably not complimentary).

The Los Trios soon disappeared. I was inconsolable, as it was the nearest I ever got to shagging Shakira. I don't remember getting home; Ben said I bowed and apologized to the band, and everybody entered a wailing wall competition. By morning, I was more relieved to have survived my fishy tale, rather than lost the Malvinas.

CHAPTER 11

In search of the goose's palm

"Life's like a box of liqueur Chocolates"

Part One

"Stop panicking mum," said Dave.

Dave, a comedy channel in himself and leading player in earlier chapters, was our real life minder, a hybrid of McCann and Arfur. If you needed a fist or a ticket for the Cup final, he was your man. OK, he has a weakness for Export and Engerland but under his Shrek exterior he was softer than a pit bull washed in Lenor.

He assured his mother again. "Look, mum don't worry, Simon knows the orient like the back of his hand." She had just learned that eight of us were off on a jolly across as she romantically put it, Indo-China.

I was rather flummoxed at Dave's statement. I looked at my watch to check the back of my hand for the Asia a-z, shit a new liver spot. Admittedly I'd been to the far east thrice, and Leytonstone for the football, but I would have hardly said I had the rickshaw knowledge.

We were about to depart on a boyz only vacation; all join in for cowboys and Indians, no girls or wives.

Six of us were departing in the morning and planning to meet up with two others later. We had all allegedly grown up together and were well into our third decade of life's rich tapestry. But if I'm honest, we still hadn't quite fully grown out of our shoe size.

That was except for Dennis, who was forty plus and from a far off northern outpost.

I had spent the early evening fighting my suitcase, as it had refused to close. It finally submitted after I suffocated it with my sixteen stone frame while wrestling its mouth shut in a scene reminiscent of Crocodile Dundee. I had just arrived to drop it off at Dave's house, the taxi collection point for the following morning.

"She's just worried mate; especially about the Vietnam bit," said Dave.

"Don't think we'll be climbing hamburger hill mate!" I said.

"More like the beer hunters," joked Crowman, another fellow traveller.

The Crowman

No relation to Worzel Gummidge and not to be confused with another mate, Rooky. Crowman dressed off a medium to large coat hanger. His frequent appearances in the Chronicles of Narnia proved to be good training for hiding in my hotel wardrobe in the hope of seeing what the butler saw. He based his psyche on Victorian children, i.e., often seen, but not heard. But he was usually chirpy today. Oh, and the only person I have ever met that ate his Mothers' Pride toasted one side.

"I realise that love," interrupted Dave's mum. Who despite her contrived act of being unworldly was in truth quite astute "Look you boys may appear mature on the outside, but most of you still can't wipe your bottoms. And as a mother I don't want you getting lost in the jungle and having to be rescued by that um, Rocky Bilbo chap."

She let out a chuckle, then added deadpan "Or your dad."

"Er, think you're searching for Rambo, Barbara," I said. "Unless they made Rocky 26 the Fellowship of the Ringer, where he fights a Hobbit."

"Don't worry Mrs H," said Crowman, continuing with our cheesy sitcom sketch. "There'll be no rumble in the jungle, in fact, I doubt if we'll ever leave the bar."

"I remember that fight Crowman," said George, Dave's dad, enthusiastically. "That was Cassius Clay v Smoking Joe Frazier, and in Zaire if my memory serves."

"You mean Ali, George." Corrected Crowman. "And I'll think you'll find it was Foreman actually, not Frazier, the one you're on about was the Thriller in Manilla," He added.

George was a foreman at Vauxhall Motors for forty years, Barbara proudly commented, "but he's never won a fight against me."

Bentleys Bar, London Heathrow October 15th, 1995.

"You scab," said Dave; I was wearing a black baseball cap (the correct way round) to hide the scorch marks on my head I had self-inflicted with a Superdrug peroxide kit.

Dennis chipped in, "You're supposed t' dye it first, and then shave it, ya twat." He said in his Yorkshire accent.

The Northerner

Dennis, a Werther's original cigar-toting plumber with a well hung perpendicular. Adopted by us southern softies, slightly, older and bolder with a real six pack and ring pulls through his nipples. A no-nonsense Corgi registered pipefitter from Ripon but not to be trusted with your Yorkshire fittings. He genuinely lived in a bat cave and had a cat called Arthur.

"I think it looks alright Simon." Remarked the other Cat, our mate.

The Cat

A small domesticated carnivore, Felis Domestica, bred in a number of varieties. Our variety wore a tortoiseshell track suit and went by the name of Colin. He somewhat resembled Bagpus in aviators with a receding hairline and a flap in his arse for strays.

Chris, our final player, returned from the bar with six more Stellas.

Ding dong, flight 902 with Thai Airways to Bangkok is now ready for boarding, will all passengers please make their way to gate thirty-three.

"Better lap up lads," meowed the Cat.

"Don't bother," I said, "the queue will be huge, and it's only a four-minute stroll."

"I'll get em in then," said Dave.

"E-Dave lad, steady on, no more chuffing Stella, I want t' remember my holiday." Complained Dennis.

We just made it. Four off us strung out like marathon stragglers took our turn to collapse at the gate.

At check in, the Thai Airways agent had informed us that the flight was to be a no smoking. So we had puffed out Battersea power station before leaving the bar. Add to this the six pints of loony juice, and a cow pie breakfast, all equated to a four-minute stroll from the Armstrong/Jackson ministry of silly moon walks.

Unfortunately, gate 33 was twenty minutes away, and our stroll became an army training run with full kit. It nearly killed us. Meanwhile, Dave and Chris sat with feet up tapping their watches as I unpacked my ventilator. Somehow they had blagged a lift from one of those annoying flashing, dancing and all beeping, make way pond life, (I'm more physically challenged than I look) people carrying buggies.

The Cat, The Crowman, and Dennis had collectively collapsed in a heap and were glaring at me with fixed bayonets. Dennis took a gulp of air and wheezed out, "That four-minute stroll you mentioned Simon, where it wit' Roger Bannister?"

The flight made a tech stop at Copenhagen; This is an airline ploy to fill up the half empty seats, that and the flight deck needed a fag break. The lads soon joined the crew with other passengers and plumes of smoke filled the air, then a fog horn sounded, and it was time to reboard.

The flight itself was pretty uneventful unless you include drinking, gambling and Chinese torture. The latter after we suffered noise pollution from the over-excitable people's republic occupying row 31 C-G. Big Dave had decided to pacify their racket by sticking his face between their seats and growling like Godzilla. The result was ejector seat practice for Ms May Ling, as her head was posted through the bulkhead. Followed by her lunch.

After we landed the usual mayhem ensued as five hundred people clambered for their bags. I've never understood this; You cannot get off until the airbridge or the buses arrive. So why do people feel the need to start climbing over each other like it's the Harrods sale? Next we had the mobile dawn chorus; It's like I must text someone and tell them 'Hoorah' I made it through the Bermuda Triangle, and mother can you check if I turned my goldfish off.

As we queued to deplane, we then received a probably deserved onslaught from the anti-snoring brigade. Who stated to the cabin crew that if we were on the same flight back, then we should be slung in the hold like pigs. Bloody hell, they've got some sauce! Probably Apple.

The old airport, Don Mung in Bangkok, was a bit of a dump, but it had kind of chaotic charm not like the new soulless Suvarnabhumi. I miss the strange gift shops stuffed with man-eating insects and the cast from Mongoose v Cobra, a far more interesting souvenir than a box of orchards, and more menacing than a straw donkey.

We boarded coach C with its Kuoni Holidays sign in the window for the twenty mile four-hour journey. I had warned the lads the Bangkok traffic moved slower than Dennis up a chimney. Today was typically slow; we inched along surrounded by a few old Toyotas, several ox carts, hundreds of tuk-tuks and thousands of mopeds, oh and an elephant from jungle book with a red tail light. We sat for sixty minutes viewing the gridlock around us. Chris Rea should have come here I thought. A loud squeal on her microphone accompanied the rep as she stood up.

Her first attempt came over as a Thai version of Jack Douglas as the microphone splattered and crackled, then it settled down.

"Hello, elly bloody my name is Gai, that mean chicken in English," she announced. Muted acknowledgment followed. "So solly Bangkok traffic velly bad and very slow, is lush hour.

Welcome to Thailand, the local time is eight o'clock."

She then wasted her bilingualism by chucking in a few hello's in Euro-lish to coach loads of Brits. This was followed by a ten-minute talk on the history of Siam, which made the cat's ears prick up.

Our fellow travellers' eyes were heavy, and I noticed they started to nod off. Then a loud blast of feedback had everyone head butting the bag racks.

"OK elly bloody, first I teach you some Thai words OK. We say hello good morning first. So For man in Thailand we say, Sa-wat-dee khrap."

Titters broke out. "Yes, I know velly funny in English, but not mean same like poo or substandard."

This statement brought out a big laugh more for the surprising second word. She carried on. "Now, please for Lady, we say Kha, Sa-wat-dee Kha. Please, now we practice together OK. Elly bloody 1. 2. 3, the response was half of half-hearted. Please, she continued, "I know you tyre, but please try join in, is holiday yeah." She repeated "This time in Thai again. Nueng, Song, Samm."

This time, she received a Bruce Forsyth reply. "OK good, now lady say Sawasdee khar."

Again a whole-hearted reply.

"Velly nice lady gentleman." She applauded wildly, which woke the driver up. She then went on to explain the usual stuff, i.e., trips, the money, the weather, the food and the pitfalls of being a tourist.

Then finally she really got on everyone's tits when she finished with "Elly bloody know English people velly generous, so please give driver tip. Yes, his name Bot, my name Gai."

With that she finished. "Thank you, Khop Khun kha."

She clasped her hands together in what's is known as a Y, and then brought them to her nose. "Please now you sleeping, but not you Bot." This brought her the biggest laugh of her gig.

After an eternity, we pulled up at our hotel, a pocket-sized green building called the Jade Pavillion. The name was nicer than the hotel, but it had a bar, a tiny pool and clean rooms with hot showers and a great view of a shanty town.

Within ten minutes, most of us had shit, shaved and showered and were pacing the pavement outside with hands deep in pockets like Christians waiting for feeding time.

Eventually, our lion, the Cat, strolled out wagging his tail.

"What's up?" Said Dave.

"Couldn't get my suitcase open, I forgot my keys and had to fucking break it." Moaned the Cat.

"Should've put it on your collar." I said.

"Right, lads, we got loads of time," I announced, "and remember people. As the rep said, no tuk-tuks, no tailors, no markets, no bars and no ladyboys. Well, at least until we get our bearings."

It fell on deaf ears as within minutes we were in two tuk-tuks, one yellow, one blue. The drivers rubbed their hands in anticipation, as we clung on and the grand prix began.

Like lambs to the slaughter, we set off for a day of drunken debauchery and general foolishness.

The first incident was when our driver, Sak, took paddocks corner too quickly. We flipped onto our side and crashed into a soup stall. Luckily sally's army were at prayers, and nobody got hurt, except for Sak's pride, which had a few dents.

Tuk-tuk number two screeched past with Chris, Dennis and Crowman giving us the Harvey Smith. Dave, in his wisdom, decided although he had never even seen a tuk-tuk, let alone driven one, that he would reverse it and proceeded immediately into a klong, (a small canal). This was quite a feat considering there was no reverse gear. The driver was rather pissed off.

"Oh fuck, sorry mate," said Dave. "I had a Lambretta once; you know same same."

"This Vespa copy," said the driver, soggily. "Not same same."

We collectively dragged it out of the klong. Luckily it was still serviceable, Sak kicked it in the bollocks, and the two-stroke rattled into life and off we wheelied, smoke pouring from the back.

Bangkok traffic back in the day was like driving through a bonfire and after half an hour you could feel your lungs burning. We were hemmed in on all sides, and as we swerved amongst the traffic holding on for dear life it was like being in a video game. We just closed our eyes and hoped Sak understood Atari.

First stop was a tailor's shop. "This my friend Mr Duck." Said Sak; "He have nice suit, I get you 25% discount, OK boyz."

We piled in the doorway and got stuck straight into the free Singha beer on offer. We spent two fucking hours getting measured up for something I personally didn't even want. The tailors were Indian, well they fronted it. We all ordered suits and shirts; Dave insisted to the annoyance of the tailor that he wanted England football buttons on his dinner suit. This added forty minutes of confusion.

"Can't you have Toggles?" Said Chris.

"Bollocks," replied Dave; "I'm not fucking Paddington."

As the afternoon wore on more beer flowed, and so did our bladders. I felt sorry for Tattoo the tiny Thai-Chinese man who was the double of the midget in fantasy island. He did the measuring up and seemed to like cupboard's, a bit like Crowman. Anyway, it turned out it wasn't the W.C., as we mistakenly thought. Undeterred Tattoo appeared from under the material and dried his hair and then produced his magic tape, running it up between our crutches like a ferret. After deposits had been left, we left, on tilt!

I remember thinking I must get some food, but the temple was next, but not any old Temple, The Grand Palace, well worth a visit. We smoked up and piled out and then bowled in only to be stopped by Friar Tuk-tuk waging his finger, "No Hat, No Glass, No Shorts and NO SHOES" He bellowed.

"What about cats?" Asked Chris.

"Er sorry, your reverence," we bowed and curtseyed and reversed out into the road.

Sak said "No problem. You can buy from my friends,"

and pointed to a shop that had conveniently made its fortune from unprepared tourists. So there we were, all dressed up like Hinge and Bracket. We wandered about the place like a troupe of tea pickers. . . and to think all that fuss about Beckham a few years later in that Sarong, I claim copyright. It did us a favour, the time being used to sober up.

The temples were impressive, especially the reclining Buddha. We did a few chants of Harry, Harry, inhaled some incense, lit some candles and re-recorded Sergeant Pepper.

'With a little help from my friends', I climbed aboard the tuk-tuk. "What's next Sak?"

"Now we see go my friend's restaurant, very nice food, I get you 25% off, bargain."

Got a lot of friends this bloke!

The restaurant was more like a zoo, you chose your creature and then it was carted off for last rites. The waiter came with the menus, smiled, placed them on the table and returned ten minutes later.

After our clueless perusal, he said, "So what you like sirs?"

"Er, got anything that's dead?" Asked Crowman with a touch of sarcasm.

"No wully, we kill for you," laughed the waiter.

"In that case, six bowls of tomato soup please." Said, Dave.

"Ah joking man, Sanook Mac Mar (very funny). Listen you want try house special?" Said the waiter.

"What's that, elephant's arse on toast?" Said Chris with another touch of sarcasm. (Well, I think it was).

Chris

The sensible one, well sort of. A second generation paddy and our peace envoy and cultural attache. Had a known Alka Seltzer habit that often got his mouth into trouble. A bit of a tubber, but stouter with a wide Beamish which gave him an overactive libido. If he had ginger hair he would have been called Duracell, OK he couldn't play the drums, but he fucked like Thumper, the rabbit.

"No, we no have elephant plate, too small!" Came back the waiter.

Good joke son, this guy was a stand-up. He continued, "We have house special, Goose' Palm. Velly nice."

"Come again lad?" Said Dennis.

"Right," said Dave, taking charge. "We'll have three goose's' palms, crispy OK? Three swans beaks, two turtle doves and a partridge in a pear tree. Please."

"Please," said the waiter, "solly no have swan. He enquired, Swan is big white bird, yes?"

"Yeah," said the Cat.

"But we do have er, how you say. . . Heron." Said the waiter.

"Jesus," we said in unison.

"These ain't the birds I came to Thailand for." Said the Cat, almost coughing up a furball.

"Just bring us a meal for six, but not too spicy and we'll leave the rest to you."

"OK boss," said the waiter. "You want pay together or one bill?"

"Er isn't that t' same?" Said Dennis.

"No problem boss, I take care you," he cheerfully replied.

Dennis laughed, then on his return asked him a question. "Excuse me, young man, how do you say, in Thai language, no problem? Oh and what's thy name?"

The waiter thought for a while and said, "We say, sir, 'no problem' and my name is Um."

Dennis enjoyed that one, Um continued. "But you can say, 'Mai me bannhar.'"

"You what, Um?" Said Cat.

He repeated slowly, "Mai-me-bann-har."

We all repeated, "My meat banner! Any good Um?"

"Er, maybe you stick wiv no problem."

Of course his answer required the combined reply of, "No problem Um."

"Any brown sauce?" Added Dave.

"Vell funny guys," he said to himself as he went off chuckling to probably piss in our soup.

Suddenly, we were surrounded by fit looking women in traditional costumes with fingernails borrowed from Edward Scissorhands. After five minutes of ogling, we were invited up to do the coathanger dance and almost immediately made cunts of ourselves.

"Soup ready" said Um, the waiter. It was Tom Yum Goong (Prawn spicy soup), and it was fucking spicy. Years ago when I had first visited Thailand in 1982, I was given a handful of bird chillies to chew on, within seconds I combusted with more flames than Joan of Arc. I couldn't speak as I breathed fire for fifteen minutes before being slain by St George.

Thai food is very popular now in the UK, but back as in the late '80s early '90s it wasn't that readily available. Just like early Indian restaurants, the food served had little to do with their traditional fodder.

We finished our soup; sweat beads ran down brows and with the hanging tongues of dogs, we lapped up Winalot in noodles, well that's what this Aussie reckoned who was behind us.

Next came a multitude of small dishes from the movie *The Temple of Doom*.

I told everybody, "Now don't pick, it's rude, just get stuck in."

The lads looked at each a bit apprehensively then dived in. Crowman was first to finish.

"Well, that was the dog's bollocks." He announced.

"As I said before." From the Aussie.

The bill was settled. We thanked everyone for their excellent hospitality and Dave popped 300 baht (£10), which was also three days wages in Thailand back in 1995, into Um's hand. Um, who had finished his shift and now had changed into a fake Liverpool shirt, bowed to each and every one of us and repeated, "Khop Khun Marg, khrap." (Thank you very much).

"Wad he say, wad he say?" Said Cat, Musky style.

"Dunno," said Chris, "probably, sorry for pissing in your soup."

We fell into our transport and spluttered off in the direction of Pat Pong, the infamous bar area at the time in Bangkok.

Still feeling the effects of a twelve course, we decided to walk the famous market for an hour but made a rule.

"Absolutely no buying, we'll come back on't last night" instructed Dennis.

Back in those days, there were still a few good bargains to be had, and the copy stuff, although a novelty, was more interesting than a mini coliseum ashtray or bullfighting poster.

Chris started to bargain hunt for some bamboo cutlery.

"Oi, it's 8 pm Chris, WTF you doing? You're not carrying that around all night." Ordered Dennis, as entertainments manager.

"Just trying to get a good price mate, for Friday."

Chris spent the next twenty minutes telling the stall owner, in pidgin English, his life story. She loved him like a lost son, and like most Thais enjoyed a joke with him. The general rule of bargaining is that you start at half price and pay no more than two-thirds or what you think its worth. He opened his bid at 10%; Her face changed from the nice old lady to the wicked witch of the east. She called him every name under the sun and more, she put a curse on his family and basically told him a cigar smoking piper would befriend his kids, and lead them off into a cave.

"So you know Dennis then?" Said Chris. We all legged it.

The first bar was a riot, full of U.S. sailors, who, in their drunken stupor, were taking on Thai kickboxers in a small ring in the centre of the bar for $10 a pop. The place was heaving with an unbelievable atmosphere, there were creatures of all descriptions, it was a bit like the bar in Star Wars, as skimpily clad women and fuck-knows-what gyrated in all directions. The music was pulsating and within five minutes the Thai boxers had demolished half of USS Gobshite. The next guy, a huge black man, was knocked clean out of the ring and landed on our table, scattering the glasses and stools everywhere.

"Sorry guys." He mouthed.

"My meat banner." Said the Cat.

We were politely moved to another table at the back, but after thirty minutes of being manhandled by Danny La Rue, we decided to sway to the next bar as big bird from Sesame Street was also approaching. The next bar we reached was a huge go-go bar. By now we were all shitfaced. We sat up at the front where the pole dancers slid up and down thrusting their wares for purchase. Then a ping-pong show began, followed by Marlborough tricks, a fake lesbo act with a bit of neon art painting. Then it was a shift change over, as twenty more twanged up hookers slid up and joined the fire brigade.

Guns 'n Roses Paradise City kicked off, accompanied by strobes and green lasers, this became all too much for Dave. So he decided to strip off into his y-fronts and join the girls on stage. At first they were a bit taken aback by the presence of Hulk but warmed to his Saturday night fever routine. Suddenly, and alarmingly, a rush of security had him bundled off the stage.

"Oh shit," I thought, not here mate, I hope I'm am not the one who's gonna be ringing Barbara for Rocky Bilbo's number. Luckily they just calmed him down and made him get dressed. In fact, the girls had quite enjoyed his show, especially when he swung his maggot to Meatloaf.

The rest of the evening became a blur; I remember Chris saying he had just been blown in the toilets, and Crowman had shit himself and couldn't find any bog roll.

Part Two

The next minute I was waking up to the sound of dogs barking and with a cracking headache. The clock said 11.15, and then I realised it was upside down and was 5.45. The Cat stirred.

"What time did we get back Colin?" I said.

"Er, fifty minutes ago!"

Fuck, what a day, what a night! I thought. "We better get up mate. The trip's at six thirty." I said.

"So what happened Cat?"

"Well," he said. "We took you home in the tuk-tuk around threeish."

"What about the others?" I enquired.

"Not sure," said the Cat. "I think Dave drove home on a giant vacuum cleaner, I lost Crowman after he went to wash his gusset out, and Dennis and Chris were perving with two bar girls."

It transpired Dave had borrowed the cleaning ladies' industrial hoover and rounded them up through reception and around the hotel, culminating into a good old British farce i.e., Run for your life! Luckily Dennis had let them out of the broom cupboard after he arrived.

Chris had taken home a new friend and had murdered her in the toilet! Well, that's what Dennis told us at a bleary-eyed breakfast. I think, realistically, Thumper may have overloaded her as well as being a bit of a tight fit.

This morning's trip was the bridge over the river Kwai, and although looking forward to it, we weren't looking forward to the long coach journey. The trip is still worth doing, even nowadays, as you still get a feel of the real Thailand. A combination of a boat trip, a train journey on the death railway and a visit to the Japanese prisoner of war camp including the immaculately kept war cemeteries. A full on day.

If you remember the film, you will probably know it was shot in what was then called Ceylon, and bears little resemblance to the real place. In fact, if you ask the Thais where Alec Guinness is, they'll probably reply "Solly no Guinness, just Chang."

We left at around daybreak more hungover than an Oliver Reed shooting party.

Another snoring match soon took place to the understandable annoyance of the rest of the tour. Then the Partridge families rudely woke us up with complaints of ear ache. Being gracious we acknowledged their complaint, but after careful consideration we instructed them to either get on board with the double deckers or fuck of back to the little house on the prairie.

After twenty-two panadol extra, we reached the boat quay. While waiting for the long ride up the river, we purchased some silly hats and a crate of hill tribe refreshments from Shackmart by the water's edge.

I decided on a pith helmet, Dave chose a law-enforcement officer's hat, the Cat went for a new collar but Dennis, not wanting to play, purchased a Nike cap. Meanwhile, Chris already had a pigs head in his bum bag.

Crowman metaphorically borrowed it by refusing to buy a hat because we were all wankers, and he could handle the 45-degree sun.

By eleven am we were starting to liven up, so Cat got the round in. Several cans of Klosters, (a German pilsner). The first one was hard work but by the time we reached the bridge for docking, a thirst had kicked in. First stop a postcard shop and then onto lunch, six large Chang's beers served cold accompanied by some triffids at the local salad bar. Then time for the bridge walk as we posed and took the customary pictures. Next on the agenda was the train ride.

We climbed aboard; our carriage happened to be full of Japanese tourists, a bit strange, I thought, considering the whole place was focused on the barbarity of the imperial army. It was the same when I visited Pearl Harbour, full of Hirohito vets. Back aboard the Kanchanaburi chu chu we got chatting with two twenty-something Honda Idols, who incidentally were wearing save the turtle t-shirts, I remember thinking the back probably read, 'for our lunch'. Their English was surprisingly pretty good. Dave's headwear had put him in character. He decided he was from the Hague and told them he was going to interview them regarding historical war crimes! Yes I know, nice one Dave. The next ten minutes was taken up with questions on "How many people did your dad torture in the war?"

Yep, cringe time. The amazing thing was they took no offence and answered quite thoughtfully and reasonably comprehensible.

Apparently, his name was Kendo Nagasaki from the Nissan rifles. The end scores on the doors were a casualty list of Tally-Ho-Kaye with a submission, a hundred minky whales, and Bobby Charlton thrashed Tenko, then escaped to Victory.

OK, maybe I exaggerated about their English.

Dave wrote out a speeding ticket and told them to have a merry Christmas with Mr Lawrence.

They bowed and thanked him, folded the ticket into a Swan and ate it.

So picture this. Six buffoons sitting in a jungle clearing huddled on a log. The Thais had put on full spread with a BBQ. But we sat feet up and petrified of the giant insects from B-movies that had us surrounded. Bees the size of hobnail boots swooped on us, ants the size of small children nibbled at us and a fat arse snake hung in trees like Khan from Jungle book.

"Don't look in his eyes" I shouted.

We didn't get to eat due to our cowardice, and we named it Hamburger Hill. Most of the other tourists loved it. Payback time for English scum. We were all nervous wrecks by the time we reboarded the coach.

The Brady Bunch particularly enjoyed our chicken shit performance. After a visit to the war graves and prison camp, we didn't arrive back at the Jade until 8 pm. It had been a long day, and Crowman had a face like a Baboon's arse and spent the night lying in a bath of aftersun and cucumbers. The rest of us showered and met up at Denny's bar, about 100 metres down the road. Denny's had become our local, and the girls loved us as we were, well basically out of control, all in a nice way you understand. Oh, and we spent shed loads.

The next day we met at ten in the hotel bar. Dave was asleep outside in a giant potted plant. Feeling like death, Chris dished out Alka Seltzers all round that only made us feel worse, and sent Chris hurrying to the Hong Nam (toilet). After we had all formed a chain reaction of honking in the Hong, a huge storm rocked the bar. We decided to retreat for a Thai massage this was a traditional massage, not a happy ending, time for that one later.

We were dressed in pyjamas and were laid out on mats. Like giggling schoolboys, we tapped our feet out to the soft sounds of the Thai supermarket music as we lay apprehensively. The curtains were suddenly pulled back and in strolled five bruisers. We were expecting exotic beauties, not Widow Twanky and the Ugly Sisters.

Well stone a Crowman, it turned into an origami come

wrestling match. We were yanked, pulled and pushed, walked on, bashed, scratched, stretched, rolled and folded and tied up like a kipper. After two hours, we resembled several pairs of wrung out socks.

The worse bit was the feet, spontaneous maniac laughing broke out as they masseurs pulled off our toenails, one by one. It was all too much, and then the Cat pissed himself. Other punters came to look what all the commotion was about.

The cat was led away like a nursery child to change his pyjamas. The masseurs were unfazed. They had seen it all before, including several stonkers that switched on every time they massaged the groin area. I was desperately thinking about ironing a French pleat to switch off my horn button but to no avail. Dave told me he was thinking about coconut Hobnobs, but Chris said, "Fuck it; I was reliving last night."

Feeling battered but relaxed, Dave let go a huge blaster. This had the Thais running for cover. It then set off another chain reaction as Blazing Saddos began. After the mist had cleared, we all stood up, in unison hands clasped, bowed, then paid over a handsome sum.

We decided to head for a haircut while still sporting our pyjamas. Our next preschool prank was to get shaved, all over. The next two hours became a sitcom; we had to split up as by now the laughing was causing serious pain. The Cat pissed himself again and was led off to buy a litter tray.

When we got back to the Jade, the staff were in fits watching Benny Hill, the prequel to Mr Bean and loved throughout the Asian world.

Forget Boy bands. We were the first Boy Buddha band. Dennis, who had returned earlier to the hotel, passed us in the lift and didn't even recognise us. But Fellow guests did, and we had now strangely become celebrities. I remember Dave posing for a photo with an Indian family who thought he was Buster Blood Vessel. (Lip up Chapati)

Later that night we visited Lumpini Stadium for some real Muay Thai (Thai boxing). It was all very exciting and intriguing as the crowd switched sides between the red and blue trunked fighters, like flicking TV channels on a remote. However, it soon became apparent it was all to do with betting. The terraced hordes were frantically swapping bets, a bit like the stock exchange; it was complete chaos to us.

We watched Claude Van Dumb defeat Mike Thai-son, then got a bit bored, so we moved on to Cabbages and Condoms. At the time, this establishment was a famous Thai restaurant that used all profits for the fight against HIV. We had to settle for green curry as they had no goose's palm, to the annoyance on the next table of Rubber Johnny. We decided to hit Nana, another bar area and more riotous behaviour ensued.

Day five was the floating market trip. So it was up again after less shut-eye than a bullfrog (apparently the only animal that never sleeps), which I can concur, on rainy evenings it's Paul McCartney's frog chorus. The trip to the market turned me into an Imodium junkie, but I somehow managed to make it to the shit house with unsoiled undercarriage. After the Market, we visited a semi-real rural Thai house, and although it was obviously staged, you got the idea of simple living pre-IKEA. We stood in the house, Dennis noticed a gun on the shelf and asked if it was loaded.

"Yes." Replied the man who owned the house.

The next conversation was translated through the rep.

Dennis, "Do you have burglars then?"

"No, it's for shooting monkeys!" The Partridge family were distraught.

Then the next minute as if on cue a monkey grabbed Dennis's leg through the floorboards and pulled him over. Dennis collided with the Cat, who in turn knocked Dave over. The whole place just cracked up, Especially David Cassidy, Who shouted to the ape, "I think I love you."

The second from last day in Bangkok we just hung around the pool drying our livers in a vat of Andrews. That night a quiet, uneventful dinner came to pass, and we turned in early.

As midnight chimed, I was disturbed by a phone call from room 407. It was Dave, who had decided that he needed some boom-boom. I arranged with Ting Tong, our bellboy, a midnight dash to the local short time palace. Dave instructed the mamasan with explicit details of his requirements, i.e., one with a silky arse, please. He ended up taking back number 32 to the hotel (that's her number, not a takeaway). Apparently she had a wooden eye and left it in his fruit bowl.

The next morning at breakfast the eye did the cereal bowl circuit then around 2 pm a storm blew up. It just hit the city from nowhere, bringing a tree down by the pool and sending everything swirling around like a mini tornado, Including my bedroom roof. I called down for maintenance but in miss understanding I was brought toast and tea by loom service.

After the power and my roof was restored we went for our last day session. We started in Denny's again but for some reason we forgot to pay the bill. We hadn't gone there with this intention, it just somehow slipped everyone's mind. By the time we had returned to our hotel, it was late afternoon, around 5 pm. Bollocks, we agreed, OK we should have paid it, but it's too late to go back now. Besides they've had about a grand (£) from us. Plus, "It was only ninety quid," remarked Crowman.

Chris wasn't happy, Rightly, I suppose, explaining the staff would get a kicking from the boss and would be made to pay it back from their salaries.

At around 7 pm, I was getting showered and packed for our departure to the airport and our onward journey to Phuket, when my room phone rang again. "What's up now Dave?" I thought.

So I answered with "Listen mate, no time for silky arses, wooden eyes, false beards or plastic tits... Use your right hand."

There was a slight pause, and then a girl's voice I half-recognised spoke. "You, Mr Simon? This is Nam from Denny bar, please, you come back bar and pay bill or have problem."

The call caught me cold, and despite my efforts to change into an ageing mumbling Italian, my fake Don Corleone accent was fooling nobody.

I pulled the line out of the socket. I wasn't sure how that would protect me from the Spicy Girls, but I had to do something. After ten minutes of planning my escape from the window, there was a knock on the door. "Oh fuck," I thought, as I had only tied two sheets together. I reluctantly and gingerly opened the door. PHEW, it was only Dave.

He explained he had also received 'the call' and despite his best attempt at Omar Sharif, it hadn't impressed the ladies.

A hastily emergency meeting was arranged for my room. Then there was a further knock on the door. Ting Tong the bellboy stood at the entrance and worryingly informed us some gentlemen were in reception, and they were requesting a little chat.

Three large notes representing the monies owed were placed under Ting Tong's hat, with instructions to offer remorse and negotiate our lives for a healthy tip. In other words, do a bit of arse licking. So off he went only to return but with bad news.

"Solly sirs but men say not three thousand baht, now is ten thousand."

"Fuck me, that's a three hundred sovs," said the Cat, playing on his currency converter while chasing a ball of wool.

We all agreed that a new plan was essential.

Chris got hold of the bellboy and stuffed a month's wages in his top pocket. Then asked him if he could smuggle us out the back into a getaway taxi. He agreed. The Cat was then sent down, after losing the vote and because we knew he would always land on his feet. He did the boy scout walk out to check our escape route and hand the keys in, as we had already weighed in the mini bar bill etc.

Also, the gang would be unsure as to what the Cat looked

like, as he's only appeared briefly in Denny's bar. But just to make sure we camouflaged him with Elton's sunglasses, Dennis's baseball cap and a plastic rabbit's nose from our bags of tricks. We gave him clear instructions.

"OK Cat, no more than five minutes and don't get killed by curiosity! Or get lost again." Which he had a knack of doing.

You may have seen his posters up on local lampposts.

It worked, the bell boy duly obliged, and we were smuggled through the underground car park and out to the airport in a taxi for 25 quid, that's £4.20 per head. Literally.

We arrived at Bangkok domestic airport with a surplus of four hours created by our mission impossible extraction, so we decided to go for a wander. We crossed the main road and entered an old railway station, come fish market. We soon found a bar/cafe shack and ordered a round.

"Yen Yen. (very cold)" I said in my best Thai to the culinarian.

He pointed to an old chest freezer where we found buried under a mountain of mullet and half of ton of melting slush, an amazing find in a fashion similar to Howard Carter! Eight bottles of ancient frozen in time Strongbow cider. It must have been there from at least Pharaoh times. We slumped down amongst the toothless locals.

"Surely it's time for dinner." Commented the Cat.

Um "OK, six goose's palms please," said Chris to the old boy banging on his cooking drum kit.

"Eh?"

We gave him a piece of paper with the translation.

"Mai me, kin blah mai? He replied (sorry, no have, eat fish mate?).

We passed around the cider on our table and to a local guy who was eating a bowl of condensed sludge. Dave engaged the man in a hands across the sea conversation that involved smiles, nods and hand gestures he borrowed from close encounters of the third world kind.

An exchange was made, vintage apple juice for a spoonful of his lunch.

Dave's smile was suddenly transformed into a wide mouth frog as the chilli kicked in. This bowl was filled with the Devils sweat. For the next twenty minutes, he fought for his breath and his life. His nose and ears started foaming like an old Hotpoint; Then after a further five minutes, his amphibian transformation was completed. His tongue had popped out like an inflating dingy, his eyes had exploded onto stalks, and he had a nice shade of putrid gills.

The locals lapped it up, even better than Mr Bean.

After much croaking, we started to get a bit worried. Chris, being first aid trained from his days in the Irish sea Scouts. Slung a bucket of iced water over Dave's head, then administered rudimentary CPR.

Dave spluttered back to life, wearing an expression of old coyote after an Acme explosion. The gathered crowd, fifty strong by now, clapped and cheered. The local man stood up and patted Dave's back while he wobbled, still punch drunk. A vat of Singha was ordered and a straw for Dave, who went and sat by a stagnant pond with his new family. By the time we reached the terminal, Dave had become pugnacious and a snorting bull. Coffees were ordered all round, and then Chris spied a Burger King and off we marched.

"Five big macs, my man." Said, Dennis. "Oh sorry, slip of tongue. Five-flamed grilled meals, please."

The staff were still trying to decipher broad Yorkshire when Dave went on tilt mode, again! He decided in his befuddled state that he would be the new manager. He made a snake line and headed off behind the counter and immediately put on a spare apron and silly hat and took over, to the bemusement of the staff.

"Right you lot, I taught Colonel Sanders everything he knows." He announced on the microphone. "Who's next?"

The rubbish dump was in his element again. If we were the chaps from Auf Wiedersehen Pet, then Dave was Oz, but with cleaner underpants.

Two customers approached to order. They turned out, unfortunately, to be Germans. We closed our eyes. Please, not the Stan Boardman impression Dave.

"Yes, who next please? Well, come, on come on." He beckoned from his platform.

Even worse, the Basil Fawlty (don't mention the war FFS.) The Germans gave Dave a frown but ordered their meal.

"Ve vant two Voppers meals, pleaze."

Dave, "Do you want Coke or Blue Nun?"

"Vot? Ve vant 2 Vopper meals vith vun grape juice and vun sprite PLEAZE."

Dave repeated back on the microphone. "Right, so that's two choppers, an ape juice, a spitfire, oh, and four sunbeds."

Dave then threw a few scoops of chips and orange juice on their tray, told them it would be 8,000 Bahts adding "bitter", and fell backwards.

The Germans just stared in utter contempt; the crowd were indifferent, some laughed some frowned.

"What are you, some kind of clown?" Said one of the Germans without the comedy accent.

"No that's McDonald's." Said Dave, from the floor.

The real manager appeared on the scene and was not amused. He apologised to the Germans and then turned to Dave and reprimanded him for his behaviour in his perfect English.

"You leave now Sir, GO, it's not funny, very unamusing, this is a business, not a game. I will call the Police."

Dave then fell over again and knocked a two hundred box display of paper crowns flying, then jumped up like nothing had happened and waved to a now hundred strong and swelling audience.

We managed to grab him before he collapsed again and dragged him away from approaching old bill and hid him in the toilet, where he fell asleep for an hour. Dennis apologised to the manager with tales of sunstroke and soup, but he was surprisingly uninterested.

We boarded the flight to Phuket. Dave was paralytic. Bear in mind this is 1995, when the airlines overseas were far more relaxed than nowadays, in fact, we were all pretty rat arsed. Dave ordered half a bottle of brandy, downed a quarter, then promptly fell asleep. At last, an hour's respite.

Part Three

On landing at Phuket airport, it took us a good half an hour to wake Dave up and with the help of the obliging flight crew we jointly lumped him off. We loaded up our taxi, which was a mini bus and wedged Dave in the front seat so he could have a bit more room to snort.

After ten minutes of general team dozing, the driver broke the silence with "Sa-wat-dee khrap, my name is Moo. Do you come to holiday Thailand? Do you like girl and boom boom, jiggy-jiggy?"

"Oh yeah," We replied slightly unenthusiastically, as we were tiring of this same old conversation.

He continued his well-worn introduction. Funny enough he knew nice girls, good tailors, nice restaurants, etc. and his list lasted two kilometres.

"Look, Pal, just get us t' hotel." Said Dennis, bluntly.

After about thirty minutes of going up and over dusty hills. Dave awoke, he opened his piss holes in the snow and looked around to get his bearings, then looking over the edge of the road, and the drop, started singing they'll be bluebirds over the white cliffs then abruptly switched his song to "Excuse me driver, why is everything green on this island?"

"Mai khao jai," said the driver (I don't understand).

"Well, mate, why are all the lights, cars and towns green?" Said Dave. "In fact, the whole place is green, are we in Greenland?"

The driver thought for a while, and working out his English replied, "Mai (no), not gleen, Mr you looking through sun visor on windscreen." You had to be there really, but it was the look of realisation on Dave's rubbered face that cracked us up, including the driver who nearly drove us off the green cliffs of Dover.

Phuket gave us time to chill out man! The first two days were spent lying around the pool like a herd of pregnant sea cows. Evenings were non-eventful as we just hung at a Swiss bar across the road recharging are batteries. On the third day we filled our backpacks with cheese and cloth and joined the hippies on a pilgrimage to Phi Phi island where I got the idea to write a book called the Beach, unfortunately, I lost the transcript, and the rest is history, oi! De Caprio, pay up.

The next two days were filled with paragliding, jet skis, scooters, elephants and accidents. Costing us a small fortune in a compensation sting operated by the vendors in conjunction with the old bill. We also attempted sea canoeing but got stuck in a cave due to our expanding waistlines and had to be rescued by the local Troy Tempest in Stingray.

On our last night, we set off for a huge jolly to Soi Bangla, Patong, the main drag on the Island for mongering. The night was a giant cocktail of alcohol, women, beggars, aggressive tailors, snakes, parrots, lion cubs, more tailors and Wimbledon vs Newcastle, Oh, and the human bottle opener trick (always knew there were other uses for a woman's front bottom).

We returned to the hotel about 2 am, the Cat with his new pussy in tow. Back in the day, quality hotels would fleece punters with a charge called a "joiners fee," normally around £20, to bring their shag into the room. Having said that, it did stop a lot of pilfering as the hotels had hold of the girls ID card.

The Cat had decided to take his stray to his room, but his first attempt was unsuccessful. He tried to sneak her past security without paying and was subsequently rugby tackled by Robocop. Unperturbed, he decided the thirty quid needed for her to pass go was now a necessity as he was on heat. By the time he got her back to our room, it was about 4 am.

I had already ablutionated and was half snoring when I heard them enter. I opened one eye and spied his kitten shuffling past my bed and into his cat basket. My abiding memory of that night is of a silhouette of an Asian beauty, lit up through the French doors by the silvery moon, gently rocking up and down on his manhood. With the Cat still wearing his glasses I might add, staring straight up at the ceiling as rigid as an ironing board, while pulling a face like a gurning champion.

Virginity broke at thirty-three? You never know. When I awoke at six, she was gone, and the cat had got his cream and was purring in the shower. Not me. I had a serious hangover and struggled for an hour to get dressed and pull my suitcase to our airport taxi.

Not much was said on the flight to Vietnam, especially after reading about a Vietnamese Airways Tupolev that had just crashed in Phnom Penh.

On arrival at Ho Chi Minh airport, we stood in line at passport control, waiting in turn for Charlie to rigorously check our visas. After about an hour, we had all made it through except for the Cat, who was being questioned about something. He was then ordered for some unknown reason to stand in a red circle in the middle of the arrivals floor.

Hundreds of tourists filed past the troubled Cat, who was wondering, as were they, what dastardly deed he had committed. Our rep, named Tiger, managed to negotiate the Cat's release from detention, but no reason was given.

We stayed in a reasonably priced four-star French hotel, which was comfortable and well-positioned downtown. However, they may have had a swanky restaurant but the French chef's carte de jour was hardly Two Star Michelin.

The first evening Chris was served a whacky races salad that was hiding the ant hill mob, Crowman ordered a crepe Suzette, not to be confused with a brothel creeper. I plumped for Hannoy Haddock that had more bones than a dogs garden and Dave had tomato soup that consisted of hot water with a tomato taking a bath. Dennis, being sensible, went for the club sandwich, but it splintered his teeth.

The next day we did the tunnel tours. They were interesting, but tight, it's strange how even now the propaganda machine is still functioning. We listened to their rhetoric and just smiled, unlike a fellow group of GI Joe's on a nostalgia trip.

The next day was a trip up the Mekong, which brought back flashes of countless movie moments from 'Nam films, including Dave's mum's mate.

Our rep that day was a cracking thirty-something sampan hat wearing Julie Andrews, who decided we looked like we were in need of an hour long surreal karaoke singalong of British nursery rhythms. Mind you, we happily endured her Ba ba black sheep, as she had huge tits that danced around more than we did.

That night we hit downtown and the Apocalypse bar.

As we approached, the excitement grew. We had conjured up an atmosphere of opium smoking Vietcong sharing a pipe with a few old Nn-nn-nineteen platoon vets. They would be sitting amongst shot down helicopter parts and Sam missile casings while slowly nodding their heads to *White Rabbit* blasting out of the sound system.

Well, what a fucking major disappointment to see a bright orange Mediterranean chill out lounge vibrating to the spice girls ziga zig-ar-ing.

We immediately shipped out and marched into next door's Aussie Steak House and set up position. The food was quite passable, and the napalm cocktails were spot on, but we decided to retire earlyish because Charlie were all blokes. On the way home we were suddenly confronted by the local East end football crew a.k.a the Saigon Inter Slitty firm, who for no apparent reason bombarded us with bottles and old plates.

At first we ran from our ambush but then we regrouped at the intersection, and in a reconstruction of the battle of Dang Na, we fired back coconut shells while singing You'll never take the Oak Road (Luton's old end). But, like John Wayne, our lines were eventually overrun, and our ammo was exhausted, like us. We fell back on Zonda taxi mopeds and retreated into the night.

On day three we decided to shoot our Tiger and his official tour bus and do a bit of business with the local rickshaw taxi guys outside our Hotel.

"Alright mate," said Dennis. "Listen pal we wanna do t' war museum, and can thee give us a bitera city tour?"

"No problem boss," said their spokesman, who we named Rick.

"Only one dollar, OK Boss?"

"One dollar for everyone?" Repeated Dennis, amazed.

"No, each cart sir." Replied Rick.

"OK, you're on." We all naively agreed.

They stuck to their word and feverishly pedalled us to the war museum, followed by the market, city hall and a few beer stops along route. At the end of our tour, we pulled up around fiveish. These guys had been chauffeuring us around for about eight hours.

Chris remarked, "Listen, lads, give em a good tip, they've worked their pedals off."

We all agreed, what a great day. We had got on very well

with the guys and for once had been model ambassadors for the UK.

In our appreciation, we decided to give them a ten dollar tip each, sixty bucks in total. As we handed over the money they morphed into Transformers, "No, not sixty dollar." Said the new Rick, "Not enough."

We laughed, and did a bit of back slapping, I offered my Robin Williams impression with "Five days in Vietnam, and my best friend is a V. C. THIS WILL NOT LOOK GOOD ON A RESUMÈ!"

They were not impressed. "You give $600, then go." Said Rick!

More Goodnight Vietnam, really. So now the price was six hundred dollars!

Crowman spoke first. "How the hell has six dollars gone to six hundred dollars? What do you think we are, fucking stupid?" (Answers on a postcard).

The arguments continued, but they were not up for negotiating. Being clever, and probably being a tried and tested scam, they had dropped us in fucking no-man's land that was about two clicks from the safety and our hotel.

We hastily arranged a meeting. First Dave said, "Look, give em twenty each."

I glanced over at the six drivers and noticed their ranks had swelled to twenty-five, some armed with sticks, metal pipes and a machete.

Dave approached Rick. "Look, Mate, we only got a hundred and forty between us, will that do?" Being ever the international diplomat, he added, "But we are not happy about this, you fucking gook, you've stitched us big time."

But Rick wouldn't budge. Dave returned looking pensive but also angry and gave us the SP.

"Right said Chis, We gotta front this or we're horse meat." We all looked decidedly apprehensive.

"OK listen, this is the plan," he continued. "We charge them shouting and waving our arms, and they will fuck off, believe me. "I ain't no stupid fucking greenhorn; these cunts are full of shit."

I rapidly pointed out that millions of very well armed Yanks had had their arses kicked, and although football battle-hardened, having it with Chelsea was hardly in the same league.

But Chris was adamant, so with the battle cry of For Harry and for Luton and St George, we lined up across the road like Pat Garrett's men, picking anything that came to hand. The tumble weed tumbled as my guts rumbled. Then Crowman arse stumbled, as our all out assault completely backfired. They met us and just piled in mob handed.

Where where the choppers? I kept thinking, "Medic" I called out, as shots rained down. Then it all became a blur as I was repeatedly paint canned over the head.

Then amongst the emulsion, music to my ears; police sirens. Three Tourist police jeeps screeched to a halt and their contents piled out; the rabble dispersed in all directions. We dragged our arses up, regrouped and surveyed our dead. None luckily, just cuts and bruises, and lots of brush marks.

The old Bill asked, in so many words, "What the fuck are you doing behind enemy lines."

We tried to explain, but they just took us back to the hotel, where Tiger was waiting to give us a serious dressing down. Suffice to say, we were just a bit dented, like our pride, but on reflection someone could have died.

Bali couldn't come too soon now, so the last day we stayed in the hotel, all giving Chris an ear bashing for his failed military campaign.

I have been back to Ho Chi Minh and Hanoi many times since. Vietnam has now developed into a serious holiday destination with great beach resorts, but like anywhere, you must always keep your wits about you.

Ten hours later we arrived knackered in Jakarta, Indonesia, then transferred to a small plane driven by the Red Baron, who battled Snoopy all the way to Denpasar, Bali.

Bali, in general, is a very nice island, but if you want a chilled out retreat then Lombok, it's sister island is a better option IMHO.

We had picked a hotel about fifteen minutes from Kuta, the Magaluf of the Island, which on an average night resembled the MSG kicking out, as Bali is the Majorca for Australians. The Balinese are very friendly people and with it's mainly Hindu population it has a very different feel from most of the other Indonesian islands.

The first thing to say about the place is it has some of the most persistent hawkers in the world. We had only been playing for ten minutes with our bucket and spades on our black volcanic beach when watch sellers surrounded us. These guys had their names emblazoned across their carry cases like Johnny, Stevo, Mick and Phil. A couple behind us from Brisbane remarked. "I don't believe that's their real names!"

Most of the timepieces were the usual cheap shite, but a couple of Tags and Rolex's were passable. After browsing ten thousand watches in Bangkok, we were a disappointment to Johnny and his mates, as we already had an arm full. Not deterred, one guy called Larry (we renamed as Snap-on because of his protruding socket set of purley's), followed us around for two days, like a dog with a stonker. Everywhere we went he would turn up, further discounting his fakes.

We would tell him "Look Snappers, $25 is way too much for a Christmas cracker Breitling, go away."

However, every two hours he would spring up somewhere else with "OK, OK, only $15 Boss."

On our white water rafting trip, he even turned up on the bridge, overhanging a Seiko for $12. Then again outside a large volcano, when he disguised himself as a pile of lava then erupted with a special offer of two Omega's $20.

On our the last day, as we were lunching, he appeared again. This time on the back of a clapped out moped, with defeated face. "OK, Boss." He pleaded just $6 my friends, any watch, I surrender. I need money for the mechanic."

"Why, are your teeth broken?" Came the reply from the Cat.

We felt sorry for him, and rewarded his persistence with twenty billion Rupiah, roughly a $20 tip. Keep your watches Snap-on, and treat yourself to a filling and a bottle of Bintang (Bali beer) we told him. He went away as happy as his case name . . . Larry.

As it happens, in the airport on the way home, Dennis admitted to buying two watches. So we all decided to come clean and laid them out on the floor of the bar. Sixty-two watches in total, copies of every make. Add those to the eighty-odd from Thailand all meant that on our return, WH Samuels would be shitting themselves.

We didn't like Kuta that much, as I said, it was like stepping back to being eighteen in Benidorm; Admittedly it was OK for a beer and we did visit Paddy's Bar and the Sari Club, the two properties tragically bombed a few years later. The rest of the Island had some magnificent scenery, and our hotel resort was majestic. We took many trips, the standouts being a white water rafting adventure and a climb of Krakatoa's little brother.

The whole experience of those few weeks can never be surpassed or even equalled and will live legendary in our memories forever. In my opinion, you can never revisit or recreate a great time. Mainly due to developing countries and changing resorts. Add to that personal circumstances, age and liver condition, but more importantly probably due to the fact we may have grown up a tad.

One last occurrence that amused me was on the way back from to Denpasar airport. The coach stopped at an official government souvenir shop. The Cat, who had resisted all trip from buying any tat from street sellers, wanted a carved wooden mask to go on his wall. He wanted me to accompany him inside as I was "a top barterer" as he put it.

He had enjoyed my collection of tat I had collected around the world which adorned the walls of my living room and often commented on it. In reality, Dennis was the best barterer, in fact, the hawkers normally ended up paying him to take it off their hands.

We entered the shop, and the Cat was immediately impressed by the large Garuda bird face mask hanging in pride of place in the shop.

"How much, please?" He enquired.

"720,000 rupiah." Came the reply.

"Fuck me! How much is that." The cat asked me.

"About sixty quid." I said.

"Oh that's alright then, I thought it was in the hundreds."

Unfortunately, his currency converter had melted on the beach, and his maths were about on a level with Frankie Abbot from the Fen Street Gang.

"Sixty pounds, that's a lot," I commented. "I got a similar one for 15, OK not official, but it looks identical."

"Na," he said, "I don't want some shit off the road, this is very good quality and made by a craftsman."

"Well, up to you Cat."

Mr gullible had it wrapped and boxed, and they even tied a bow around it. The Cat then cradled his souvenir for the entire flight home, guarding it with nine lives.

Two months later on visiting his house, I asked where the mask was, as his wall still had the obligatory painting of Warhol's Campbell's soup and his mum's bequeathed three flying ducks.

He grunted in reply. "It's in the kitchen; the fucking cheating spanner mouth bastards did me."

"Oh, you're joking, I said," trying not to smile.

"Yeah, they switched it on me when they wrapped it, it's just a fucking block of wood."

I walked into the kitchen and collapsed with laughter.

"Yeah you can laugh Simon, but I got the last one. The bastards won't get me."

He had only gone and given it pride of place and drew two eyes and a beak on it.

CHAPTER 12

Anchor What?

My last chapter contains a story that with a spoon of Tarantino could transfer to the big screen. I've already got a cast in mind. I just need Oliver Stone's director's chair, Hitchcock's cigar, an apocalyptic soundtrack, plus Lottery funding.

It was that time of the year again. Yep, another visa run from Thailand, this time I had chosen Siem Reap, Cambodia, for my three-day mission.

Cambodia, for a while known as Kampuchea, is the keeper of the 8th wonder of the world, Angkor Wat. It was also home to the Khmer Rouge, who in four years wiped out a quarter of its people just to reinvent the calendar. Their attempt at genocide won them the Axis of Evil Red Ribbon, just beating

Stalin and the Nazis, who we were finished off in a dead heat, thus leaving the Rwandans with the wooden scythe. The North Koreans were disqualified for assassinating Bambi's mum and replacing her with a new deer leader.

In the airport bar, I was befriended by at a group of Millwall supporters, some might say a contradiction in terms! We stuck a conversation about Thailand. I couldn't help noticing one of them, who was named Woody, wasn't quite the full ticket. I asked one of his pals, "Is your mate OK?" As he was standing behind a potted Palm fiddling with his flies.

"Yeah, geezer," came the reply, "don't worry he's alwight".

"Oi, Woody" Shouted another friend. "What the fuck you doing, you muppet?"

The guy I was chatting with, Dan, confided in me. "Fucking nonce, I fort he'd stopped doing that".

"Oh is that his party trick then"? I asked. "Naa, he was born with half a sandwich. . . He kept doing it back in Bermondsey, kept hiding in wood with his prince in hand having a mash every time some ol trout walked past, but I fort he'd knocked it on the 'ed."

"Got nicked by the Bow-street runners did he?" I joked.

"Oi Son, we're sarf London, not Cockney West Ham cunts, and naa, he fell in a fucking bramble bush!"

I boarded my flight to Siem Reap slightly hesitant because I had been told by the girl at check-in that I may have "trouble on arrival."

Her concerns were to do with my passport, which

contained more visas than my wallet. A lot of Asian countries issue stupid stickers that fill up your passport like a Panini album. Mine was already full.

I had pondered my dilemma, then foolishly decided to remove a previous Cambodian visa. Why I didn't pick an Indonesian, Singaporean or some other one, I'll never know, but it turned out to be a grave error of judgment.

I had argued with the girl at check-in that a bit of green stuff under the counter would normally smooth over iffy ingress with tinpot territories. She argued that as a plan, this was a highly precarious, and it could result in a long stay in a cell with Glitter. What does she know?, I thought, I was a seasoned campaigner with over million flights, I'd even travelled through the middle east from Tel Aviv dressed as King Richard, even Dynamo couldn't pull that off. Time for the gameshow big X.

We touched down, and I disembarked and joined the queue towards several dozen uniformed men sitting at several uniformed desks. Removing my hat and shades I tried to look touristy.

This is the part where you present your passport, two photos and 25 uncle sams to receive your Visa. My immigration guy was your typical mechanical miserable official. He stared at my passport like he was stuck on pause for ten minutes then he moved his hand and repeatedly flicked through it like what the butler saw.

Suddenly he stood up and slapped the book down on the

desk and looked up disparagingly. "Why YOU take out old Cambodia visa?" He shouted.

Searching for some bullshit, that wasn't forthcoming, I looked towards the Bushwackers (Millwall) for backup, but then again they'd already stitched me with their wanky story. They collectively shrugged.

"Err, sorry, I replied."

He started to prod my chest. "But why Cambodia?" He continually quizzed me. I could tell it wasn't the removing of the visa that had turned him assiduous but the fact that I had chosen to expel his hallowed turf.

He then ordered me to stand aside and wait in the corner. I wrote a D on my hat and placed it on my head. "You fucking Idiot." I thought, as I apologised to my conscience. A new guy arrived who had extra go faster stripes on his epaulettes, but he just turned out to be another clone, who repeatedly asked me the same question. "Why you take out Cambodia visa?"

I reached into my bag for my humble head and switched on my defence. "OK, OK, look I'm very sorry, but I had no more space, I only realised on the plane, it was a genuine mistake. I love Cambodia guvnor, honest, I just sorta peeled it off, sorry officer."

He gave me his best lingering hard arse stare and then scribbled some stuff down on his notepad before policing off. I stood by a mini temple and entered into another hour of repentance with Buddha and any other God that who would listen.

THE SEARCH FOR THE GOOSE'S PALM

Then the torture squad turned up, cuffed me and escorted me into detention

The next few hours were to be serious squeaky bum time. Don't tell 'em your name Pike! The inquisition began and lasted until I passed out on my bed of nails after they attached electrodes to my testicles, and tickled my feet with a giant feather.

The door squeaked, and I woke up, checking my watch; fuck me, I'd been here for four hours. The door opened and in shuffled an old woman from 'Dinner Ladies'. She plonked a wooden cup of water and a small pastry down, but with no file inside. Eventually, the door swung open again, and to my surprise the firing squad didn't appear but Fred Scuttle. He minced up to the small wooden table I was sat at in the middle of the room. He was wearing a full-length military coat, a beret, wire-rim spectacles and a dopey expression. He sat down, then offered me a smoke. I declined. He lit up, opened his clipboard and Introduced himself as some kind of judicial prick, which I didn't quite understand as my Khmer was rusty.

He then proceeded to rattle off an array of questions on all sorts of subjects; he didn't even look up. Some of the questions were totally irrelevant to my detention and although shitting myself back up by the turtle head pressing its way between my cheeks, his English pronunciation had me smirking.

Question 8. "Tell me Mr Gleen, you like wimmin?" Fuck me, it is Benny Hill again. "Yes, I prefer the sea." I answered somewhat confused.

Right! I thought I'm getting bored of playing fucking seventies TV, Time to construct an inoffensive defence.

Deciding to go straight for my summation, I said "Look, your Honour, I've come here to see the splendor of Angkor Wat and other Temples, not Shirley Temple. I don't even like girls, well, actually I do, although I've nothing against gays of course" . . . Oh fuck I'm digging a hole again.

Hi Ho, Hi Ho, it's off the gaol we go. Oh, this is fucking hopeless. The turtle made a break for it.

"The defence rests". I sat back down and squelched.

The door opened again and this time in walked Hills Angels. Not really, it was the cavalry, the Bangkok Airways rep with a cheap suited and ill fitted western official. Feeling a complete twat, I said to her, "I hear the humble pie is very good in Tuol Sleng prison."

"Pardon, sir?" She replied.

"Err, that's an apology I guess." I said.

She frowned; the suit turned out to be Frank the Yank from the US consulate. He told me that the big cheeses were extremely pissed off with my criminal damage offence, and they would probably deport me, or maybe even charge me for defacing the King's property. He continued that this charge can carry a five-year gaol sentence, but they were still mulling it over.

Suddenly, my bollocks blocked my windpipe, and my life flashed before me, I gulped like Tom the cat "Can I choose the first one?"

To cut a long story short, and not wanting to sample their version of Spandau, I proceeded to bury my tongue deeply up several of the brasses arses. I grovelled like Kunta Kinte with the old slave routine, pleading, please don't whip me, boss, don't whip me, master, I'm too young to die. In truth, I apologised regarding my offence firstly to Scuttle, and then a table full of brass chaired by a man wider than taller, a Major General Short Crust.

He listened intently to my flakey statement then stood up, walked over and without taking his callous black eyes off me stamped on a cockroach; then he bent over right in front of me and stuck his arse in my face as he picked it up. He turned his head back, with his mince pies still transfixed on mine. His Leer reminded me of a sex case on a bus who once tried to entice me with milk gums to get mine around his plums when I was fourteen. "OK, I wanted to leave like a bat out of hell," I thought, "and I'll do anything for that, but I won't do meatloaf."

It was eventually agreed that I would write an official letter of apology to the Prime Minister and pay a fine involving a couple pictures of Franklin Benjamin; After all the hullaballoo I really should have just got the fuck outta Dodge, but then I was struck by an idiotic Eastern proverb. 'Barking dogs seldom bite.'

"No, fuck it," I thought. "I've laid out a good wedge for my hotels, trips and air tickets, etc. So I'll freewheel this situation." When I got to my Hotel, I had a shower, a cup of green tea, and then slipped into my predator suit and fused with the jungle.

Later that night, after being blown up by Schwarzenegger, I repaired myself with the sewing kit from the bathroom and took a cab into town just for a few beers, only for medicinal purposes you understand. I should have ordered a milkshake to match my hand tremors, as the gravity of the day had by now caught up with me. I sat at a cafe in Drinking Street, downtown Siem Reap, with my government tag sitting across the road. He desperately needed training in being inconspicuous, but then again maybe his plan was to intimidate me into being the model tourist.

I sent him over beer, á la Eddie Murphy in Beverley Hills Cop. Drinking street has a few bars and discos that are frequented by hippies and backpackers but I wasn't in the mood for jovialities.

I drunk up, donned my cap to Johhny Cambodian and went back to my Room and read my Lonely Planet brook.

It was around 11 am when we pulled up outside Angkor. I surveyed the entrance from my window.

"Em, think this Hotel needs a bit of work!" I joked with the Driver.

"Solly sir this, not Hotel, this Angkor." He replied.

I paid him and left him on a retainer for the rest of the day as it was a long way back to basecamp. I traipsed around for a couple of hours.

Yeah, granted, all very impressive and all very cultural and Discovery channel. So Please don't get me wrong, I'm not a philistine but after thirty minutes I was feeling rather bored meandering around this giant sandcastle. So I bought a postcard and a stick of rock, then left.

I know some people spend weeks looking around it and marvelling at its splendour and majesty, but being honest regarding ancient wonders, given the choice I'd rather hang at the garden bar in Babylon.

I returned to my hotel, then haggled with my taxi man named Nib, a price to Phnom Penh. My plan was to meet up for a beer Lao with an English teacher I knew, called Rab. He used to sing in a UK punk band, and I had met him a couple of years ago on a previous visit.

The far east is full of English teachers who probably haven't got a GCSE between them, but for a few bucks you can take a TFEOL course, It's not quite entry standard for Yale, but it's a way of extending your stay by getting a visa, although the pay is pretty lousy.

I already knew how the day would go. We would meet in a small Irish bar and would talk about the old days. Then we would put on sounds of the late seventies and get shitfaced.

1,2,3,4, I set off in the cab at 2 am, while the government spy slept with a banana up his exhaust. That night we went through three road blocks that cost me another $50 US. I kept thinking, "For fuck sake; most backpackers stay for three months on what I'd spent in only three days." We Pol Potted along, reaching Phnom Penh eight hours later. The new motorway seemed to have been built from ox shit with blue-bottles for cat's eyes.

Phnom Penh is the vibrant bustling capital of Cambodia. Situated at the confluence of three rivers, the mighty Mekong, the Bassac and the great Tonle Sap. A city once considered the 'gem' of Indochina. The capital still maintains considerable charm, with plenty to see. Well, that's what the travel guide will tell you. In reality, it has a lot of poverty but does exude a sort of provincial charm with French colonial mansions and tree-lined boulevards amongst monumental Angkorian architecture. Oh, and several hundred shanty dwellings, the usual beggars and moped graveyards.

As I said, Phnom Penh by day is a pleasant enough place, with markets, parks, French bakeries and temples aplenty. By night, it is a different kettle of contrast, with poorly lit streets due to power shortages.

However, many new western style restaurants have sprung up downtown, lining the banks of the Mekong River. This has become the place to be seen for affluent Cambodians wishing to sample expensive wines and mingle with five-star tourists.

Take yourself a five-minute walk and you'll find yourself amongst the alleys and back streets with seedy bars that still have an air of lawlessness and an uneasy atmosphere. There is tolerance for the tourist, but I never felt like the Dead Kennedys, i.e., meaning that I wouldn't probably holiday here out of choice even in a Kim Wilde video from her heyday.

I checked into the Whisky & Beef Shank Hotel and gave Nib a good tip, and a new pen. He had become my faithful companion like a version of Dith Pran from the movie The Killing Fields. I gave him a hug and told him."With these roads mate, you better trade your Toyota with Professor Pat Pending."

I had researched my Phom Penh hotel in a fossil fuel powered internet shop back in Bangkok. It was the first hotel I came across, and as the pages turned slower than a giant pancake, it looked a bit rising damp but I decided it would do. I entered the small foyer of the hotel with my medium bag and was greeted at once by the large owner who introduced himself as Rod. He was I guess in his late thirties, and I'd say and by his accent, an Aussie.

We started chatting about the usual things, like where are you from? What do you do? Rod told me he was ex-forces, a commando. He had soldiered all over the world for the green and gold with the emphasis lately on the gold. He did indeed have a sort of craggy mercenary face topped with short sandy hair; He took my bag, I noticed that his toned forearm had a tattooed map of S.A. and Angola. I could visualise him at work.

He showed me up to my room, He was wearing a Mambo surf t-shirt, famous in Oz, khaki shorts and canvas combat boots, so I named him Rambo, what else! The room was a fairly bland in yellow with high ceilings a large fan and a tiny TV. The plaster was hanging for its life over my home welded bedstead. I threw my bag on the mattress and pulled out my toiletries (see picture on the cover). I then turned on the air con by opening the window, and decided to take a shower with my bugging roomates under the water can.

I met Rod again at 7 pm in his bar, and we sat and watched Super 12's rugby on live sat feed. An Australian team, the ACT Brumbies, won the title, His mates, lookalike actors from the movie Wild Geese, happily knocked back Grey Goose as drinks flowed on the house. I watched the vetted locals of some standing mixing with the expats and backpackers; all were in a Jovial mood.

I also noticed how small in stature the Cambodians were, Rambo reckoned it was due to the years of poor nourishment.

The next day one of his barmaids called Chavy, showed me around the city, including the new shopping centre. She had a point of pride and an inquisitive pile of questions, including about how Phnom Penh measured up against Luton? "We gotta better midfield." I replied.

In the afternoon, I thought I'd go sightseeing. So after a quick tour around a palace, where my guide, an oriental version of Duncan Norvell, kept wanting me to chase him. I set off by cab for a horrible history lesson. S21 is a delightful institution that would give Auschwitz a run for its money. It's a nondescript building, but boy does it hold a secret.

I signed the register and noted all comments from the visitors, this building, now a museum had a harrowing past. Make no mistake, you could feel the presence of misery from the unspeakable atrocities committed here. I stood quietly in one of the icy rooms; I imagined, or maybe I could hear a painful echo from its audible walls. Haunting photos of professional people who faces had a resignation that they were about to be tortured and killed followed you around.

I realise it was kill or be killed but these heinous crimes, still, I might add, being carried out today in other locations by inhuman fuckwits, beggar belief. I set off again, this time for the fields, hundreds of skulls piled high in glass tanks and more stories awaited. It wasn't quite how I imagined it from the movie of the same name but even so, two million dead.

1800 hours 25/07/year zero plus 33. I returned to my hotel in sombre and reflective mood. Even the devil, who was sat on my shoulder was weeping.

That evening Rambo invited me out on the piss again to his new bar called Jack's Creek, a joint venture he had entered into with another Aussie. Rambo liked to chat with me at every opportunity. I think he liked me because I briefly lived in Sydney and had toured Oz, was a bit knowledgeable about the wide world, and not, as he put it, your stereotypical whinging Pom type. He also had a dislike for, as he put it again." Fucking Uni, save the planet, hypocritical scrounging cunts, on a year sabbatical". . . his main customers as far as I could make out!

The drive to Jack's Creek was in the gloom, as I said, the roads are very poorly lit, and I soon lost my sense of direction. Gangs of lurking shadows hid in corners as we passed through the lanes, and occasionally the headlight would light up packs of emaciated dogs. We joined the main road and passed some light traffic of old wrecks and a chugging tractor.

Most of the decent vehicles in Phnom Penh are driven either by the CPP, the Government, NGO's, non-government organisations or the WHO (World Health Organisation, not Roger Daltry.) The latter two mainly swan about pretending to be looking for paedo's or doing humanitarian work but, on the whole, they are having a good time at the UN's expense. Cynicism, who me?

We pulled up along the side of the bar in a small deserted street. Suddenly an immaculate Rolls Royce and a top of the range Merc 500SL whooshed past. It was probably a couple of extremely high ranking officials or maybe gangsters, same thing really.

It reminded me of a trip to Hanoi, Vietnam a few months earlier. I went to a bar opposite the Hoe Low jail, built by the French in old colonial days; this was the jail that housed Senator John McCain during the Vietnam war. He's the guy if you remember, who ran for the presidency in 2008 against Obama with sidekick Palin does Dallas.

The bar above in Hanoi had a collection of Rollers similar to the Conrad Hotel in Kowloon. There was also some vintage cars, probably stolen from a sort of Beaulieu or Chris Evans garage. Most of them are owned by fat cats or government types who were occupying most of the tables; vintage French shampoo was flowing wildly as dozens of girls offered themselves up as 15-course meals. This common behaviour seriously conflicts with the propaganda they still pump out to the tourists about the disease of capitalism. Maybe they've found a cure!

Nevertheless, it still goes on openly, while 99% of the rest of the population are still at home sewing Nike t-shirts into the night before they get up after ten minutes kip, to drag a buffalo around a field full of unexploded US bombs left from Operation Menu. Who said the world was fair, not me!

Meanwhile back in Phnom Penh. . . "Oi, come on then Simon", said Rambo opening the door.

The bar had a modest entrance with a small neon Jack Daniels sign and a flickering VB lightbox. Rambo explained as we entered, that he had a 50% share in it with his mate Jacko who was from Brisbane. It was the last thing he said though that had my alarm bells ringing. There'd been trouble last night when a local hoodlum known as Ton had overdosed on Jacobs Creek, resulting in an unprovoked machete attack on Jacko. That's great, I thought, well it's Saturday night, so let's hope he's at home watching Ready Steady Gook!

I entered the saloon; It had that Aussie Country Roadhouse feel with pictures of classic Aussie motors plus a few hubcaps slung upon the walls. Over the bar. retro advertising made from tin jostled for space amongst old sports stars from rugby league and AFL. The actual well stocked bar was square and made of old dark stained wood with a green tiled counter and half a dozen accompanying stools.

I suppose there were about sixty covers slung about the place, with a higgledy-piggledy mixture of table and chairs.

I circumnavigated the bar; it was almost empty except for the barman and a large table of characters to the left of me. I ordered a VB; Rambo, now sitting with the characters signalled to the barman that it was on the house and then asked me to join him at his table of friends. I took my beer and sat my arse down on a lime coloured bench made in the style of imitation tree bark with matching table. These, ugly painted concrete sets are often found in many South Eastern Asian bars because they are cheap and robust. I was introduced clockwise to Rambo's gang.

To my right, and sharing my branch, sat Captain Scarlet, a local lawman I'd say in his late thirties with a red cap, red T-shirt and flashing eyes. On the next bench, to my right sat the ageing long haired silverback female, no, not a gorilla, but Jules, a French doctor from Médecins Sans Frontières. Squeezed up closely to her was a Kiwi known as Haka, a teacher and a brick shithouse in his early thirties and an Islander I would guess.

Opposite me, sat next to Rambo, was Jacko the co-owner, a portly pork chop of a fellow with Merv Hughes moustache and arm in a sling, the result of last night's attack. Then occupying the last spot at the table in his rocking chair sat Jersey Jim, a seriously large lump wearing a Playboy t-shirt with pervert emblazoned across the front. He resembled Stinky Pete from Toy Story 2; the character stuck in his box, or in his case up one as his t-shirt suggested. If you've never seen the movie, maybe a better description would be Grandpa from the Walton's. "Night Jim Bob" "Goodnight Elizabeth." "Night Grandpa." "Fuck you, Mary Lou?" "Oh alright then".

After five minutes of shaking hands and introductions, Rambo placed a large green baize sheet over the table. He then skimmed a full rack of vampire tests tubes, a bottle of JD and numerous beers on a tray into the middle. He followed that up with a couple of new packs of Crown Casino playing cards. Captain Scarlet passed a joint around and then licked some suspicious sherbert. He raised his eyebrows to me like, want some? but I shook my head and the palm of my hand. Fuck that shit, although I would have had his liquorice though.

Jersey Jim rubbed his hands in anticipation, "Any food Rod?" he enquired, Rod/Rambo moved away.

"See what I can do." he replied.

I noticed he then sat up at the bar and spoke with a security guard who had just turned up for a few minutes.

I broke the ice and chatted a for a bit with Scarlet, who informed me basically that he had been brought in on a retainer, their man in Phnom Penh if you like. He had got the licences, and all he paperwork, but he was not only copper, he was also a lawyer, a baker and candlestick maker. No doubt services rendered in return for free booze and a small envelope every month. We chatted some more; I thought about turning the conversation to how pleasant Immigration where, but as it was my fault, I decided to talk the international language of Asia; Manchester United.

The cards were shuffled and dealt by Jersey Jim. Texas Holdem.

"Right it's five bucks on the flop", said Jim spying his hand. "If you're not familiar with Holdem Simon, there are four types of poker players. The tight, the loose, the passive, and the aggressive. Which one are you?"

"Err, the useless" I replied.

Just then the door banged open and interrupted the laughter. In walked another army guy with an AK47 slung over his shoulder. Cambodian dialogue was exchanged with Captain Scarlet before he returned outside. Scarlet informed me he wasn't from the army, but another hired pot shot for heightened security after last night's take away Chop Suey. Talking of food, a plate of ribs appeared and blackened chicken plus another round of beers. Texas went on into the night; it was the strangest game of poker I'd ever played, lots of cheating and arguing. Luckily I was playing to lose, $50 bucks to keep the peace, no problem.

My next memories are like mulligatawny soup in a cheap restaurant. It is best not to stir them but here goes. The call of a raise was suddenly drowned out by shouting as the door swung open again, and this time in stumbled an inebriated local with a green face. Fuck me it was Data from Star Trek. Were we in the holodeck on the Enterprise?

The green-faced man was toting a weapon. Fire crackers flashed, and bullets spewed out. I immediately dived onto the floor and started snaking towards cowards corner. More gunfire, shouting and hollering, this time accompanied by Gallic screaming.

"End program" I shouted at the ship's computer. No such luck, this was all too real.

I dived into the shit box and kicked the door shut. I was crapping myself again and running low on Y-fronts. I looked for an escape route, but the window was from a Wendy house.

After what seemed like an age and two goodbye cruel world letters, the commotion quietened down. I could hear the CD playing the Beatles, but it should have been Dire Straits. Then sirens, followed by new shouting and finally footsteps. Bang, bang, bang on my door, no not gunshots. Knock, knock, knock, no not Brotherhood of man either, but Khmer schpeel.

"Er, hello", I softly sang, Lionel Richie style as I inched open my door with my heart beating out serious drum and bass. Thank fuckish, it was Cambodian ragtag military, Major Tong and his junkies. He ushered me out with his pistol and back into the bar.

Captain Scarlet, demoted, sat sheepishly as Tong, who had

more pips, orchestrated proceedings. I surveyed the wreckage, bits of rocking chair and glass lay on the floor; there was blood all over the table or maybe it was from the smashed test tubes, I wasn't sure. I then saw Rambo crouching with his arm around Jersey Jim, who lay beached on the floor. I also could hear Jacko arguing with someone outside.

I gingerly walked around the table to get my wallet; when I saw the green man dead on the floor. . . I nearly chucked, he had more holes than a crazy golf course. I looked away; then I noticed I also had become green 'Bing', it then it dawned on me it was the glow of the wall light.

I turned to go outside for some fresh air; I had to step over another man curled on the floor who was hancuffed. Scarlip got up and walked over and booted him in the head. I made it outside, but one of the soldiers told me to wait by the tree. Rambo quickly followed and beckoned me over.

"What the Fuck was all that about?" I demanded to know.

Rambo began to explain that the guy from last night had come back packing with his pal. But he won't be fucking coming again." He said.

I made a statement to some army guy who understood less than Fed Scuttle then after half a bottle of Chivas, Rambo drove me home. I didn't sleep that night, and if I thought to myself if I were a cat I was down to one life.

The next morning I bailed out at 0600. I didn't see or even say goodbye to Rambo, I just left him sixty bucks for the staff, and to cover any extras. I did email him a few months later. He told me they shut Jack's Creek down, no customers, just a green ghost. He also told me Jack was back in Oz, and luckily Jersey Jim had survived his shooting and went back to the States for treatment, but Dr Jules had died, probably of fright. Haka was OK and still doing his teaching, and Captain Scarlet was still frequenting the Whiskey and Beef Shank for free vino and Vegemite.

A Funny thing happened as I waited for my taxi that last morning. Chavy, the Cambodian barmaid appeared. She invited me to breakfast at a nearby food stall, her treat, she insisted. She brought me over a strange soup, seemingly made from small rodents and bats wings.

"Is this Dracula minestrone?" I Joked.

"No Simon, this is, how you say?, Err, Gooses hand, very nice."

Fuck me, I'd found it!

Gooses palm! Feet if you will.

Mind you, to think the search had taken fifteen years and 12 chapters.

Was it worth it? Yeah, It was alright, but nothing to write home about!

ACKNOWLEDGEMENTS

I was going to dedicate this book by writing some amusing tribute to credit card providers. After a while I changed my mind, shifting between suppliers of items such as suitcases, aircraft and lager. Thinking again, the standard mum and dad or wife and children dedication was probably in order. Of course, I should thank all the characters who appear in the pages, especially my travelling companions. If you were there, then you know who you are.

Instead, this book is dedicated to now. You can never go back to a time or event in your life and however much effort you put in, you can never recreate it. There is only now. Now is where things happen. If you do your best to make now a bit more exciting, then later on you may have something to write about. It is always now and has been forever.